SAUDI ARABIA UNDERCOVI

Known to his friends as the poor-man's Hunter S. Thompson, Harper Walsh has spent more than a decade as a vagabond smuggler around Southeast Asia and the Middle East. He drinks, writes, DJs and avoids incarceration in your favourite vacation spots. If there was a modern-day villain to the millenials' 'influencers' Harper would be it. When not working in war zones, he divides his time between hunting vinyl and DJing, writing, dive bars and beaches.

Saudi Arabia
Undercover

Harper Walsh

monsoon

monsoonbooks

First published in 2019
by Monsoon Books Ltd
www.monsoonbooks.co.uk

No.1 The Lodge, Burrough Court,
Burrough on the Hill, Leics. LE14 2QS, UK.

ISBN (paperback): 978-1-912049-60-8
ISBN (ebook): 978-1-912049-61-5

Cover design by Cover Kitchen.

A Cataloguing-in-Publication data record is available from the British Library.

FSC
MIX
Paper from responsible sources
www.fsc.org   FSC® C018072

Printed and bound in Great Britain by Clays Ltd, Elcograf S.p.A.
21 20 19   1 2 3 4 5

For

Al Shepard and Super Duty Tough Work: The most infamous

Author's Note

The image on the frontcover implies no disrespect to Saudi Arabian women or other Muslim women or to Islam in general. The model is neither Saudi Arabian, nor Muslim, nor in fact real ... she is both virtuous and virtual.

Introduction

The Kingdom of Saudi Arabia (KSA) was founded in 1932 by Ibn Saud. Since then it has been run by his family, the House of Saud, an absolute monarchy, worth about $1.4 trillion. KSA is one of the world's leading oil producers and is home to roughly 33 million people, 12 million of them foreign workers. Saudis practice an ultraconservative religious movement called Wahhabism within Sunni Islam. They strictly enforce Sharia (Islamic law). Public stoning, beheadings and crucifixions of beheaded bodies are all commonplace occurrences in KSA. Women have only recently been allowed to drive cars. Alcohol is forbidden (*haram*). Elections of any kind are rare. It is often regarded as a totalitarian regime.

How easy is it to find alcohol?

My time in KSA started out with a coup in Thailand, strangely enough. On May 22nd 2014 General Prayut launched a coup d'état in Bangkok, Thailand. This was Thailand's 12th coup in its history. I had been working as a consultant for a large international company in northern Bangkok for the past two years. I supplemented this income DJing nightly at various clubs, hotel lounges and art houses throughout the city. After the coup, General Prayut banned gatherings of four people or more, dancing and basically any nightlife activities. In one coup my DJing gigs disappeared overnight and my income was cut by half.

I was 30 and sick of making a third-world salary. The absence of DJing not only stung my wallet harshly but also took the wind out of a fun nightlife, which had made the corporate day job tolerable. A friend of mine named Jersey, whom I had met in 2007 on the island of Phuket, was working in Saudi Arabia doing military consulting. I called him up and asked what life was like. He responded with something along the lines of: "It sucks but it pays."

My only question was, "How easy is it to find alcohol?"

He laughed and responded, "Well, the Canadian alcoholic fell out of the van wasted when we arrived to work this morning so you won't have a problem."

You may be unaware that there are few countries on our planet that have a zero tolerance ban on alcoholic beverages. KSA is one of them. No alcohol is sold, bought, made or imported (legally speaking).

With confirmation of accessible booze I decided I had had enough fun in Bangkok and needed to make some decent money for a change. I interviewed with the Jordanian defence contractor that Jersey worked for and was hired instantly. The interview was brief. A Filipino man interviewed me and had one thing to say. "There is no alcohol or contact with women here, will you be ok with this?" I assured him it wouldn't be a problem and I was on a plane to KSA weeks later.

Jet Airways was the airline booked for me, with a brief layover in Delhi. On the flight from Bangkok to Delhi I was sitting next to a younger Indian couple in their mid-30s. The girl began small talk and suggested I go to Goa because they have "great heroin". I smiled and nodded. Now I know where to get good cheap heroin should the desire arise. The layover in Delhi was the last time I thought that I'd get to have alcohol for the foreseeable future so I went to a lounge and had several beers.

The last leg of the flight into Dammam, Saudi Arabia, was quick. Only about two and a half hours. The stewards all knew what each foreigner was thinking on the flight and they kept the beers flowing constantly. Thanks guys.

Arrival in the kingdom

I flew into the Eastern Province of Dammam, Saudi Arabia. Customs and immigration at Dammam airport looked pretty similar to anything you'd see elsewhere. Long-ass lines and unhappy immigration officials slowly stamping passports and sipping tea. Conveniently, I breezed through. No visa-on-arrivals were issued for KSA at this time so all visas had to be arranged prior to arrival. Additionally, no tourist visas were issued for KSA, only business working visas and religious visas.

After completing immigration I collected my bags and waited by a Popeye's chicken restaurant inside the airport for a man named Mohammed. All I was told was that a man named Mohammed would pick me up and take me to my accommodation. I was one of only four white foreigners at the airport, so to say I stood out would be accurate. The first thing you notice when arriving in KSA is everyone is dressed in black or white.: men in long white thobes that look like satin one–piece pyjamas; women in long black burkas with 97% of them covering their face with only their eyes exposed. The only females who exposed their faces in KSA were foreign women.

A tall, dark man approached me and asked if I was there for the contracting company; I said I was. He extended his hand and said, "I'm Mohammed, let's go". Mohammed was about six foot five, early 30s and from Sudan. His English was very good and he seemed friendly enough. While we drove away from the airport he welcomed me to KSA. He said Bahrain was only a short drive away so staying in KSA would be easier if weekends were spent in Bahrain partying. "They have women you can talk to there, beer you can drink." Sounds good to me, I thought. Mohammed then leant over and said "they also have boys" and winked at me. Then he said "young boys" and double-winked. Fuckin hell. This was gonna be a great ride. I chose to nod politely and kept convo at a minimum the rest of the way.

18th Street

We finally approached the accommodation, an unmarked apartment building on 18th Street "downtown" Dammam City. It was about 3 am, the streets were not well lit and everything was very dark. We got out of the van and walked down through a back alley into a tunnel that lead into what you or I would describe as an apartment building. We took a broken elevator up to the second floor and Mohammed opened a huge two-bedroom apartment for me.

The apartment itself was more than fine. It had a large entrance hallway, living room, two bedrooms, a kitchen and a bathroom with a bathtub (yes!). The floor was tiled until you were in the bedrooms, where they had this soft linoleum fake woodprint covering the ground. The furniture looked like it came out of a cancelled Egyptian 70s soap opera. Arabs and decoration ain't well known. Mohammed left me with two bottles of water and bade me goodnight.

First morning

The next morning my friend Jersey, who got me the job, came round and took me out for food. Our first stop was the staple and highlight of Saudi culture, Kabsa. Kabsa is the national dish. Rice, chicken and raisins. It tastes as bland as it sounds, however the Saudis view it as filet mignon. You eat it with your hands. It's fine for 15 riyals ($4.50). It comes on a massive plate with half a dead chicken so that 15 riyals goes far. Now you may be envisioning several types of restaurants here. The majority of dining establishments are separated into two areas: "males" (or sometimes listed as just "singles", which only refers to single males) and then "families". Family sections are where females are allowed to enter as well as families. The entire country is segregated with basically a sign at every business entrance telling men to marry the fuck up and make more Islamic babies.

However, as with most little-known facts about the kingdom, these facets of the culture are not strictly enforced across the board. This kabsa restaurant had no family side and was more of a take-away place. Needless to say it was one of the few restaurants that wasn't split for males and females. Now 99% of the time you would never see just a group of girls sitting in there but it does exist. They are hard lined no doubt about Sharia law but it's not as crazy as Fox news would like you to believe. Women do walk and go shopping by themselves.

After eating my mediocre lunch we walked around my neighbourhood and Jersey gave me the lowdown. Have you ever seen the movie "The Kingdom"? Remember at the end when one of them is kidnapped and they drive through the city and end up in an area where "they shouldn't be"? That's what 18th Street in Dammam looked like. It was about 8 city blocks of old buildings, flat roofs, abandoned cars, a gas station, a Popeye's and various other stores that would only open at night. The end of 18th Street connected to a corniche where there was a nice aquamarine stretch of seawater. This water was so polluted from the nearby oil refineries you could never swim in it or fish. Either way it was a nice change of colour from the three years of BROWN that would come to be my life in KSA.

Looks safe

That evening Jersey and I walked to a nearby McDonald's, yes they do indeed have McDonald's. We had to walk through an empty, sand-filled parking lot about the size of two football fields. In the middle of this sand lot was an old abandoned station wagon with its windows busted out. Saudis are extremely lazy, so rather than fix their cars they will just abandon them wherever they seem fit. Don't get it twisted, they are not all filthy rich, so there aren't just Bentleys abandoned laying around everywhere. Many Saudis are less educated and lower-middle class, if that. So back to the station wagon. Upon approach we found a strange colour inside the wagon. We walked closer to inspect it and the wagon was filled with bright pink cotton candy. "Looks safe," said Jersey. What the actual fuck? After snapping some pictures we decided to leave the child-rape-wagon alone and head off for the cleanest food around – McDonald's.

First day of work

The job Jersey had got me was as an advisor for the Royal Saudi Air Force. We would train, observe, test, and suggest ways to help implement training programmes for their cadets. This was basically a jobs programme for desert kids and asshole Saudi teens, with hopes of keeping them out of ISIS and Al-Qaeda. There were about thirty foreigners on the team. A supervisor, twenty-six English teachers and four military advisors, which was my role.

On my first day I waited outside the apartment building for

our van drivers with the rest of the team. I was easily the youngest out of all of them. We took two vans with our drivers, both of whom were from the Sudan and named Mohamed.

The team had just returned from their Hajj (Islamic holiday) vacation. The Saudis don't like non-Muslims "kafirs" or non-believers to stay in the country during Islamic holidays, so most companies offer a plentiful amount of time off away from the kingdom. In all honesty you would go insane if you didn't have the large stacks of vacation. I've seen it happen.

The team

The team at the air force was a lovely mixed group of old angry men from around the world. We had our supervisor, Steve, an elderly British man who was a P.O.W. in the Iraq-Kuwait war. We had an older English gentleman we called The Mad Hatter as he had bright red hair and would laugh insanely at random times, but was extremely well spoken and well mannered to a T. Groundskeeper Willy, an old, angry, tall Scotsman. The leprechaun, an old Irishman, ex IRA, who would take his vacations to countries to buy gems and hide them in his various apartments scattered throughout Bulgaria, hence his nickname. Florida was an ex-US Navy recovering alcoholic who you will hear plenty more about in the chapters to come.

The Small Scotsman, a smaller and angrier version of Gimli from "Lord of The Rings" with the fashion sense of the late 1980s in full effect. Trevor, a small balding miserable teacher who wore crocs to work and slept most of the time. Remember Danny DeVito's Penguin in "Batman"? If the Penguin and Jack White from The White Stripes fucked and had a baby, it would look like Trevor. Trevor ate Nerds for breakfast because he found "they just really wake me up". One morning (6 am) I saw him eating what looked like old McDonald's leftover Big Macs.

"What are you eating, Trevor?" I asked.

"Meat and cheese sandwich! Why!?" Trevor had married a Filipino prostitute, who married him for a green card then left him for Vegas. Trevor was still quite bitter about this, as one would be I suppose. We had one massive Canadian who looked like a Viking. The Viking was your typical Canadian, quite nice and polite, with the superpower of triggering the Small Scotsman and winding up Florida.

We also had four South Africans, who were all the most normal of the team. Three of them were gay. Homosexuality is illegal in Saudi Arabia, but you ain't ever gonna find more gay people in any country than in KSA. Two of them were a couple, Slumdog and Cornell. Slumdog looked Indian and Cornell looked like Chris Cornell from Sound Garden. Before you go getting all SJW on me, Slumdog and I are still to this day amazing friends. He as well as others in our circle are more than OK with me referring him to as Slumdog. We both loved "Slumdog Millionaire" too, so relax.

Lastly, we had Potter. Potter was a young-ish British bookworm, who looked exactly like Harry Potter. I reminded him of this as often as possible. Potter will be appearing at great lengths throughout this book. Netflix could have a Potter show. Netflix should have a Potter show.

You have already been introduced to Jersey. Jersey and I first met on the island of Phuket when I did a TEFL course in the summer of 2007. Jersey is a six-foot-seven, 250-pound body builder. He is also one of the funniest, most relaxed and chilled people I've encountered abroad.

Fitness time

The only thing to do in our neighbourhood was to go to the gym. Fitness Time was about a 2-mile walk away, along the corniche, from where we lived. Every day the Viking, the Small Scotsman, Potter and I would walk down to the gym, work out and come home. Rinse and repeat. The gym was actually quite nice; Saudis rarely used it and if they did they were just on their phones the entire time. The gym was a nice escape from the mundane life of KSA. The pool inside looked out onto the ocean. The gym also provided lots of entertainment as the Small Scotsman would regularly freak out on Saudis there for misusing equipment, swimming in multiple lanes, moving his towel and other things normal people don't freak out about. We'd be in the shower room washing off after our workouts and we'd hear the Scotsman yell at the top of his lungs: "who dae feck moved me towel!!! I knows it was one of yous, come up now and tell us before I bash ya in ya sons a bitches!" The Small Scotsman had zero patience when it came to the Saudis.

Salah: Anytime

Salah, I must tell you about Salah. Islam teaches Muslims to pray five times a day. If you are in KSA, then Salah, or prayer time, is unavoidable. Everything shuts down. Religious police, called the Mutawa, patrol the cities to make sure businesses close during prayer time. Mosques blast over loud speakers the call to prayer.

This amplified call-to-prayer is never ending all year round. The prayer times fluctuate throughout the year and are based on the moon. So sometimes they start at 4 am and other times they start at 7 am. These absolutely suck if you are not Muslim.

Everything you do has to be planned around Salah. If you leave at the wrong time to do grocery shopping then you're stuck in a blacked-out grocery store waiting for twenty-five minutes till you can leave. So, to make life easier, everyone gets a call-to-prayer app that will tell you the prayer times throughout each day.

18th Street hood

Beautiful 18th Street. 18th Street towards the non-corniche end had an area that would awake around 8 pm at night, called The REZ. Groundskeeper Willy gave it the nickname because all the imported Indian and Bangladeshis migrant workers would come out at night and do their shopping there. Saudis would also shop there but it was predominantly migrant workers.

Saudis are night people. It's hot AF during the day. Like 130F hot. So most businesses don't open until 4 pm, if that. Everything is subsidized by the royal family so you never really see Saudis working. The Rez was filled with Indian, Pakistani, Bangladeshi and Nepalese workers. Plenty of Saudis shopping but none working (at all). During the Arab Spring it was reported in the west that the King of Saudi opened his chequebook to boost salaries, build housing and finance religious organisations, neutralising any potential opposition.

Ocular insemination

You have no contact with females at all in KSA except at the grocery store. Every grocery store that had more than three checkout lanes would employ female migrant workers. This means non-western females. They would be in full-on burkas head to toe. Face fully covered with only the eyes peering out. Jersey took me round the city and explained the importance of timing and shopping around Salah. He also told me this would be my only time to make or have any contact with females. Jersey had developed a game called ocular insemination. It was basically eye flirting. The girls would be staring at you while you checked out. Out of nowhere you had to look up at them, directly in the eye, make eye contact, which would then prompt them to quickly look away and break eye contact. You both would get a lil contact buzz off of eye contact. Jersey would say "you gotta sneak attack em". So just when they were mid staring at you, you darted your eyes up – BAM – hit em with the eyes. Ocular insemination. Practice makes perfect.

Chop Chop Square

Near The Rez was Chop Chop Square. Every town and village and city in KSA has a chop chop square. It's where the beheadings and limb amputations happen on Fridays. Our chop chop square was of particular interest because they crucified drug offenders there, after first beheading them. Walk past Dammam City's chop

chop square and you can see beheaded-crucified drug dealers, if that's your thing. All chop chop squares are open to the public, Muslim and non-Muslim. Fathers bring their children. Foreigners go to gawk and shock-and-aw themselves then usually end up leaving KSA within weeks due to mental problems. Who woulda thought witnessing actual sanctioned human decapitation would have negative mental health affects?

Popeye's chicken

We had a Popeye's chicken on 18th Street. It was an absolute blessing. The Popeye's was separated per usual: singles and families. The employees at Popeye's were all Filipino. This was also strangely the same case for all fast-food restaurants in the kingdom. Our team probably spent thousands of dollars there during our time on 18th Street. It was located directly below our apartment building. So every day after work half our team would get lunch there. The workers inside were very nice gentlemen and would deliver our orders to our rooms if one happened to be so lazy as to not be able to wait for four minutes. Well, this was true for several. By now I hope you have already guessed Trevor was one, and you'd be correct. Trevor would get two two litres of cola with his orders. Everyday. Yeah. Without a doubt. Florida would also be in Popeye's yelling at these poor Filipinos for their inaccurate delivery time predictions "DON'T LIE TO ME, MAN!!! YOU SAID 10 MINUTES LAST TIME AND IT WAS AT LEAST 13!!!" Florida needed to be calmed down and coached regularly. Enter Florida.

Florida

Florida was in his late 50s and classified as a dry-drunk. He had hit the bottle and the Bolivian marching powder hard in his younger years and it showed. He was a tall man of about six foot four, who had the sad look of a 1950s newspaper comic cartoon, a look he wore daily. He had two favourite catchphrases: "You are a scholar and a gentleman" and "Just trying to do the right thing, ya know". Florida's room was filled with self-help books. He was a nice guy but alcohol had taken its toll on him and he would just dig holes and fall in them regularly.

Being raised by a southern father and Irish mother, respect for elders was a must in my house. My first week at the air force I was sitting in the break room when Florida walked in and the rest of the guys immediately started in on him. "Hey, Florida, did you hear they're giving away fishing rods downstairs?" "Florida, did you find the van this morning?" "Florida, I'm surprised you found your way out of your mother's vagina" Just nasty, nasty comments I wouldn't even think of saying to my closest friends.

I was like, what the hell is wrong with these guys? Why are they being so mean to the old guy? After a couple months it made sense and it soon will to you as well.

Florida was a storyteller. He had no filter either. So, I can tell you Florida's explicit sexual history and timeline. Some of the inappropriate stories that would come out his mouth were as follows. On what would seem to be a normal day in the break room Florida was regaling us with a prostitution scene in South Korea. This was about, oh, the third time we had heard this specific tale. There was a famous old streetwalker he would regularly turn down on his days ashore in South Korea. She was "haggard as could be but still rolling tricks daily". Another afternoon while The Viking was egging him on he asked us the question "it's not rape if it's anal, right?" Bursts of laughter. The Viking confirmed: "Yes, Florida, it is in fact NOT rape if it's anal."

Male youth

The programme we all worked for was a jobs programme to keep young Saudis out of terrorist groups. Remember how all the restaurants in KSA have separations? Singles and families. All these guys grow up with signs everywhere saying "get married" and "why are you still single?" The only exposure Saudi males have had with women is with their sisters, mothers and housemaids (if they had one). Often their first sexual experience is with a male. Reports of girls being molested by family members are not uncommon, as well as reports of boys touching housemaids at their dad's approval and instruction. "Here's how to fuck, son, now go fuck the Filipino maid."

Imagine a 24-year-old American guy who has never kissed a girl nor even spoken to one. Awkward, angry and highly in need of physical release. Saudi men's entire life is based upon getting married. It's all they think about and it's all their families think about. The only way a Saudi male can get a wife is with a hefty dowry paid to the bride's family and a solid job. You have an overabundance of uneducated, highly self-entitled males making up the lower and middle class of KSA. The recruiters for terrorist groups offer all these guys a job and wife. "Hey, Abdul, oh you didn't go to college, you need a wife ay? We will give you a job and wife, maybe two, just come rock with us and hate n kill kafirs."

Breakdown of KSA

The country runs like this. There is the royal family. The family has princes and princesses. Like hundreds. In KSA four wives are A.O.K. All the princes get a monthly allowance. We had a prince that went to our gym. They're everywhere. Not all the royals work and many will never have to. Then you have about a top 10% upper class that is outside of the royal family. These people have family businesses and international businesses. Some with those are linked to royals, some with global companies. These people don't work ether. They employ foreigners to work for them. Then you have the rest of the country. The biggest misconception about KSA and the people is that they're filthy rich, driving Lamborghinis all day. This couldn't be further from the truth. Many are poor as shit. The royal family just subsidizes everything. They are extremely tribal people. So if you're from a certain tribe and so inclined you could find your way to a high-paying job in an oil company. Restaurants, shops, taxis, colleges, are all filled with foreigners who support absolutely every aspect of the country.

Schools

The public school and private school systems are heavily dependent on foreign workers. Here's what happens. Go three hours in any direction in the desert and find the nearest school. All the teachers and administrators are Filipino or Indian and are being paid pennies. The local families send their kids to these schools but the kids and their parents have zero respect for the teachers and staff because they're looked on as hired servants. Saudis have the most misplaced, undeserving, false sense of entitlement.

You have elementary schools where you learn your ABCs, maths, social skills, etc. The kids neither listen to nor obey the teacher because they are "the help". So what happens is the teachers just sit in the break room and drink tea. It's pointless dealing with a Saudi who doesn't want to do something unless you threaten physical abuse. We'll get to that later. The teachers don't pass the little Saudi kids 'cos they refuse to learn or do shit. Mom and Dad come into the school and yell at the teacher and threaten to send them back to their country and take away their job so the teacher then passes the student. Year after year, child after child. The students don't learn anything and have this mentality instilled in them from childhood. "I don't have to work or do anything I don't want to because my parents will just yell at people so I get my way." Self-preservation and work ethic are non-existent. The schools are separated. Male and female. This is not how a society should be run.

This happens in the entire country for much of the population. So, little Abdul Yahya is 18 and finds a college that takes mercy on him but then drops out within the first semester because homework is fucked and he's expected to actually do shit.

If his father ain't from the right tribe he therefore has no solid family money. So what's a lazy ass Saudi to do? Well there is ISIS but he hears there's not much air-conditioning at the ISIS camps. With few to no options his father will sign him up for the navy or air force. It will give him a paying job and he'll be able to get a wife and make babies and spread Islam and eat lots of kabsa and then get another wife and make more babies and spread more Islam and eat even more kabsa.

Lil side note for ya. A girls' school caught fire in KSA back in 2002. Some of the girls weren't wearing their hijabs. It was widely reported the Mutawa wouldn't let them leave the building and they died. This made international news but was quickly suppressed.

Cadets

The cadets at the air force were predominantly Bedouin. Bedouin means desert people. Traditionally a nomadic people, the Bedouin now live in cities but retain a lot of their traditional culture and are sometimes looked down on by other Saudis, much as hicks might be in the States or gypsies in the UK. Let's just say these kids were not the brightest. Their ages ranged from 17 to 24. In two years at the air force I met 3 intelligent kids. My job was to sit in different classes, observe teachers and students and write reports on their progress to the captain. Every week I would meet with the captain and go over these reports. My job was to give him advice on how to help their graduating numbers increase or at least decrease their dropout rate.

The class numbers were anywhere from six to twenty-four. The last thing these kids wanted to be doing was learning about military shit from kafirs. Their poor teachers (Potter, the Viking, etc.) had what was one of the most horrible jobs I've ever seen. These kids would spit at them and straight up refuse to do anything in class. Fortunately the air force knew these kids were assholes so they made up a system of disciplinary reports, known as DRs If a DR was issued by an instructor to a student they would spend the weekend in jail on base and couldn't leave for the weekend to go eat kabsa.

Think I'm mentioning kabsa too much? These cadets would get caught and sent to jail for climbing the air force base's walls in attempt to go into town to get kabsa. No joke.

So the DRs were a good deterrent for decreasing shitty behaviour in the teachers' classrooms. In addition to the DR, which would take some time out of the class's agenda for the day, the teacher could also call on an angel from above known as Misfa.

Enter Misfa

Misfa, or Misfir, as its properly spelled was a mid-50s NCO (non-commissioned officer) who was in charge of discipline. If a cadet was being a bastard then you could open your door and wave down to Misfa and he would proceed to physical beat and or exercise the cadet. His favourite weapon of choice was a broken broom handle that he would beat the cadets with. This was not Alcatraz, they weren't bruised or beaten so badly that it would require a hospital visit. Down the road they're cutting off limbs for stealing carrots. So if Ahkmad gets a couple whacks upside the head so he doesn't be a fuck stick all day so be it. Happily so be it. One of Misfa's sidekicks, who would also dish out wallops, was an older very dark-skinned NCO named Haroun. Haroun had the best style of punishment. He would line cadets up against a facing a wall, walk behind them and whack them on the back of their heads or the back of their hands. The cadets would instantly cry out in pain to which they'd be met with another whack and he would get right up next to their faces, eyes wide open, put a finger up to his mouth and quietly say "SHHHHHHHH!!!!!" Suffer in silence. This was a favourite of mine and others to watch.

Hushing rape

Prior to my arrival at the air force there was a rape. Yes, it is a male-only air force. As I said before most of these guys' first sexual experience was with another male, possibly a friend or relative. There's a word in Arabic for the pitcher and the catcher. If you're pitching over here its much less frowned upon. If you're catching then that shit's gay as fuck and is looked down upon and well ... harshly punished, if not executed. The rape story goes like this. A young cadet was giving some of the NCOs the fuck-me eyes. He was "putting it out there" is how it was explained to me. Several of them do actually do this. You can certainly pick out some gay cadets if you're around them enough. So this one unfortunate cadet was putting out his ass signals quite publically and one evening they found him getting fucked by several older NCOs in the shower. While the cadet might have been putting out "I-wanna-get-fucked-signals", I don't think he was desiring a train of guys ploughing through him. They all disappeared. Had they been executed it would have been public. The KSA military obviously doesn't have any homosexuals in it so this was covered up quietly and quickly. The NCOs were transferred or forced to retire and the kid was never seen of or heard from again.

Testing at the air force

Every two weeks the cadets would have to take a listening and reading exam on their current military books. All the questions were multiple choice. The teachers would normally proctor, administer and observe the test. The South Africans would grade and check them. When I first started I offered to help out the teachers with administering the test. It would only help my reports if I could see how they did during the tests anyway.

The supervisor for the air force sat me down before I did the test. He said, "They will cheat and they are very bad at cheating." The cadets would go into a computer lab. There would be twenty-five listening and twenty-five reading questions. Two teachers per room. One to check IDs and names of the cadets entering the room. One to watch them sit down to make sure they were in the correct seat. Teachers had to make sure they didn't sit in their attendance roster order because they would then plan out who was next to who, so they could rely on them for answers. So all seating was randomly assigned before testing.

New pencils had to be given out in the testing room after everyone had entered. Students had been known to make small indents on their pencils to indicate a, b, c, d for fifty questions so they weren't permitted to bring their own pencils. Students were searched and had to empty all pockets prior to entering each testing room. They would write answers on their uniforms, bring cheat sheets, anything you can imagine they would try and fail miserably.

They cheated sooooooo much that the official air force policy for cheating was a warning for the first time caught, if caught a second time the instructor was to move them to a different seat, yes I know, ridiculous. Caught cheating a third time and they were to be kicked out of the test. There were several instructors who could not put up with the cadets' laziness and lack of any effort in trying to learn and or study. They would yell and scream and kick cadets out immediately. Every morning before the test the air force supervisor would have us tell him the policy to confirm it. "We know, we know, let them cheat twice then kick them out, you need not remind us every week."

The cadets would do so poorly on these exams that the air force had two testing days. Those that failed the first day would re-test the next day. This is how bad it was there. Whenever I hear westerners talk about how lucky it must be to be born Saudi I cringe and shake my head. The outside world really has no idea. The Saudis are the laughing stock of the entire Middle East. They can't drive, they don't speak English, they don't work, they're lazy and self-entitled, the list goes on. When I'm in the States doing visa processing, more often than not my taxi driver from the airport is Middle Eastern. We will talk shit on Saudis the entire journey from the airport to my hotel.

First cadet day

Every month the air force would have a cadet day. This was always on a Thursday. Islamic countries have their weekends on a Friday and Saturday. So, with each cadet day we would get a three-day weekend. My first cadet day I flew back to Bangkok to pick up my turntables and bring them back. Plan was to fly out of KSA Thursday morning, arrive Bangkok Thursday night and party, Friday pick up my turntables, DJ Friday night, and Saturday morning fly back to KSA arriving Saturday night. All possible. Our cadet day-off was never confirmed until the day before so I was anxiously awaiting confirmation so I could buy my ticket. It was confirmed and I bought a Qatar airways flight for $470 round trip. Thanks, Qatar.

My turntables and other possessions were left with a friend of mine, Master Shake, back in Bangkok. If you have seen Aqua Teen Hunger Force, this guy is exactly like the character Master Shake. He's brutally cynical and has a knack for identifying and amplifying people's faults. I met Shake with Jersey in Phuket back in '07. What can I tell you about Shake? He was the first person I ever saw in Thailand (the only person actually) to try and fight a tuk-tuk driver. Tuk-tuks are three-wheeled mini taxis. Their Thai drivers are all mafia. Known for their short tempers and for not taking any shit from idiot tourists. Long story short, Shake was smashed drunk and didn't want to pay his tuk-tuk driver one night. So, instead of paying the fare, he suggested the tuk-tuk driver suck his dick instead. The driver pulled out a machete and tried to kill him before Shake's Thai girlfriend stepped in to save him. He's a character. A wildly hysterical character.

DMM Airport

Dammam airport is like no other airport you will ever hopefully never see. At the departure drop-off area there is a litter of Saudis and foreign migrant workers scrambling to get inside. Once inside everyone goes through a luggage scanner prior to getting tickets and checking bags. The Indians and Bangladeshis all have massive boxes, the contents of which remain an unsolved mystery.

Rest assured if you encounter a westerner who lived in the Middle East he or she will tell you about having to deal with the box-packers in line at the airports. Once your luggage is scanned you proceed to your check-in counter. Dammam airport had about three double-sided rows of check-in counters. Get tix, check luggage, immigration then security.

Immigration was relatively painless in KSA when I was there. Not all my friends agree with that last sentence. KSA had two types of business visa: the highly sought after Iqama and a visitor's business visa. The Iqama is the real deal visa you should have, the visitor's biz visa is for Daniel and Warren from Texas, who come over for a month to consult then leave never to return. The biz visit visa is cheaper and far less restricted. The Iqama requires blood tests, background checks and a good portion of money. With the Iqama you also get to do the famous shit-in-a-cup-test, twice, once in your home country and once upon arrival in KSA. Why they do this is beyond me, as KSA is by far one of the least clean countries to ever exist.

Diseases are exported not imported. So back to the visas and immigration. If your company doesn't want to shell out the cost of an Iqama then they get you a biz visa that's valid for six months with one-month exits. This means you must leave the country once a month each month for the duration of the visa. The Iqama has many movement and entry / exit restrictions attached to it. They can stop you from exiting the country and leaving all together if your paperwork isn't in order. Me? I had the business visit visa my first two years so I could hop in and out with ease.

Immigration? Check and done. Now we get to the most useless asinine section in all the kingdom and probably the world. Ladies and gentleman, meet the lovely people of Saudi Arabia and their marvellous and exemplary airport security.

Airport security

Before I go into detail about KSA's baller-ass airport security, allow me to explain just how lazy Saudis can be. I want you to imagine you are driving down the road in your nearest city, the car in front of you throws out a cigarette, a paper cup, a hamburger wrapper ... take your pick. Can you picture it? Good. The trash you imagined, did it arch when thrown away? Did it zip out the car window so as not to possibly hit the car? Yeah, thought so.

Some Saudis are so fucking lazy they do not throw garbage when they litter, they release. Their arm will come out the window and their pinched thumb and forefingers, pointed downwards holding onto whatever item that want to trash, will open like a crane at a construction site. This is immediately followed by several flicks of the fingers to expel any possible trace of trash from their holy-chosen fingers. Why release? Why not throw like the rest of the world? Cos throwing requires far too much effort. Yeah, I know. Why litter in the first place. The trash is cleaned up throughout the city by poor imported migrant workers who walk around all day picking up rubbish thrown EVERYWHERE by the Saudis.

So let's get back to the airport security. Like any other airport there was a man or two behind the bag scanner and a metal detector you walked through. Only difference was, females walked through a separate one behind curtains. Not one motherfucking Saudi would take off their various forms of metal. Coins in pockets, watches on, belts on, shoes on. They walked through, it beeped, the guy behind the screen (supposed to be watching bags) would put up his arm and say, "Hey, habibi you got to …" before he finishes his sentence the Saudi in question has already blurted out ten different complaints about how he is not going to take all his metal off and he is going to his gate. "Take off my shoes for what?" "Why do you want to see my watch? It's a watch, it tells the time." The security guard would roll his eyes and waive him through. This happenned hundreds of times a day in all Saudi airports. Only non-Saudis would ever be forced to empty everything and walk back through, and even then if you beeped they'd just wave you through 'cos what's the point? Saudi airways flies into America, UK and many other countries.

Smoking in airports

Since Saudis love to smoke there will always be smoking rooms in KSA airports. Do Saudis go in them? Fuck no, they smoke where they want. This is the same for shopping malls. Saudis will walk around smoking. So the plus side to everyone being able to carry bombs, guns and drugs on flights outta KSA is that you will be able to get your nicotine fix preflight hi-jack / explosion.

Qatar's flight went off with no problems and I had a gem of a layover in Doha's baller-ass airport. There are iMac desktop computers scattered throughout the airport and leather beds for resting peppered throughout the terminals. Doha's airport is possible my favourite in the world and you should definitely fly through given the chance.

Long weekend in Bangkok

I arrived in Bangkok Thursday night and went straight to meet

Master Shake in the city. Bangkok was still strangling itself with traffic so I took the sky train into town. Bangkok had recently gone through its most recent coup but was still a decadent urban playground, just run by a junta. Shake and I had a night of partying planned and I was to pick up my turntables from his house the next day. I met him at Phaya Thai station, a train stop in central Bangkok. He needed to pick up weed from his new dealer, a Frenchman who had recently started working at Shake's company. I met Shake at the station and we rolled to the Frenchman's condo. It was a nice two-bedroom pad. The Frenchman has just had a child with his girlfriend from England. They are both working in Bangkok with a newborn. This is not something you see in Thailand.

Foreign couples don't move to Thailand to have a baby, nor to raise one. The Frenchman sold Shake his bag of weed, we rolled up a big spliff and puffed it down over some beers. I gave them a lowdown on KSA then motioned to Shake that we needed to get our move on. I'd come straight from the airport, still had my bag, had been in airports and airplanes since 4 am, it was now 9 pm and I hadn't spoken to a female in months. We left and headed to my hotel, which was about seven stops away on the sky train in another area called On-Nut. I checked in, dropped my bag off in my room and washed my face. Shake left his satchel of weed on the desk in my room.

Soi Cowboy

I'd been in KSA for about two months by this time. No beer, no women. So of course we went straight to Soi Cowboy. Soi Cowboy is a go-go bar street in Bangkok. It's filled with beer bars, bright lights and lots of scantily dressed Thai women that dance about. We downed several beers then several more and bar-hopped around Cowboy. The females dancing at these bars would sit with you and make small talk while you bought them drinks, for which they would earn a cut of the sales. They were mostly if not all dressed in bikinis, miniskirts, etc. Not fully naked.

It's not like a strip club in a western country where girls strip and give lap dances. A girl on Cowboy might sit on your lap but there isn't any straddling or lap-dance type of things going on. So it's kind of a tame strip club with the biggest difference being that here the girls will go home with the patrons. Tips can be given but money is never thrown at the dancers as Thai banknotes have the King printed on them. Anything to do with the Royal Thai family (especially the King) must be treated with immense respect. So throwing money is a no-no to say the least when in Thailand.

These girls dancing at Soi Cowboy will go home with customers providing you pay a bar fine – a fee to the bar so the girl can leave work – as well as an agreed-upon payment the girl takes for a short-time or long-time arrangement of adult activities in a room somewhere. Niether Shake nor I were interested in what is sometimes called pay-for-play. Shake was married and I was hornier for beer than vagina at the time, and to be honest, don't know how well I could have performed with the amount of booze n weed in my system. Don't have anything against sex-workers nor the men or women who procure their services. If everybody is consenting adults and one another are treated with respect, then you go do you fam.

Alcohol and some eye candy was all I needed for the night, so we continued on our way from Soi Cowboy towards Nana. Nana is another area of Bangkok where you can find lots of women out and about at night, plenty of them club girls, bar girls, prostitutes, backpackers, hotel workers, etc. If you're looking to drink and be around girls (a lot of them) then Bangkok has three main spots: RCA (an eight-city-block section of clubs), Khao San Road (backpacker hell) and Sukhumvit Road. We were on Sukhumvit Road. At night from Soi (side street in Thai) 1 to Soi 20 Sukhumvit there are street bars set up all down Sukhumvit. Cheap beers and post-club closing hours here.

We sat down for about an hour sucking down ice-cold tall Leo beers. You have about three beers of choice in Thailand: Chang, Singha, Leo. Leo is best. Trust. It was at about 3 am at this point in time and I was stumbling hard. From what I remember I told Shake I'd find us another bar. I Irish-goodbyed Shake and foggily made it back to my hotel to pass out.

The next morning

When drinking to the point of blackout in Bangkok the next morning can be full of surprises. Mostly bad ones. Men get their drinks spiked in Thailand, not women. Today was not one of those days thankfully. I woke up in my hotel hungover as fuck but alone and with my passport and wallet intact, that's a win.

I checked my phone. It had several messages with expletives from Shake asking where the fuck I went. I messaged him and said I would hop in a taxi and head up to Rangsit where he was living and working. Rangsit is about an hour or so drive north of Bangkok in a province called Pratumthani. I used to work at the same location as Shake doing consulting, so I was happy to visit again briefly. Shake texted back to ask me to bring his satchel of weed that he had left at my hotel. Too easy.

Satchel of death

I opened the satchel to transfer his weed into my small satchel and saw at least a half-pound of weed all separated into gram baggies. That is an immediate distribution / trafficking sentence if caught. That's automatic death penalty in Thailand. Fuck ... me ... Shake was a huge stoner. He smoked weed all day long every day. Didn't think he was buying this sort of quantity though. Fuck, I couldn't fit this in my satchel so I grabbed his satchel and proceeded out of the hotel. The hangover immediately kicked in. My body was like, "Thanks for all the food and water you didn't have yesterday". Next two hours were gonna be fun.

I exited the hotel, which was directly on Sukhumvit, and hooked a left to hit up the family mart convenient store for a Gatorade to nurse my hangover. As soon as I turned left, I had about 40 feet to the family mart. I took about ten steps looking at the ground then looked up to see who was standing outside the family mart looking directly at me. A cop. Luckily I was wearing glasses or he would have immediately seen my horrified look and as I swallowed my soul.

I literally had a death sentence on my back. Thank the gods, devils, bigfoots and aliens that there was a stairwell to the sky train between me and the cop. I made a turn and slowly climbed the stairs to the sky train and made my panic-induced escape from the cop who I was praying would not take the opportunity to stop and frisk me as they regularly like to do. I got up to the sky train, bought a ticket, went through the turnstyles (oh fuck, they look in bags here) and luckily I got the usual Thai-look-in-bag-security-check, closely associated with Dammam Airport's security check. This means they don't really look in your bag but just shine a light and pretend. Gimmie Xanax and lots of it, please. This hangover morning was sucking. All for turntables. Sometimes I wish I had developed different hobbies when younger. I would then never have to be travelling with heavy-ass vinyl records and turntables.

I was so shook at this point I just rode the train to the last stop. After seeing the cop in On-Nut I quickly remembered how many police stand around the train lines and stop n frisk foreigners hoping they find one as stupid as I was that day to shake down. I made it all the way to the last stop, Mo Chit, and hopped in a taxi. Immediately told the taxi to take the tollway to Rangsit, avoiding any possible police road stops. Cops in Thailand do whatever they want. Stop, frisk, drug test, passport check, etc. They are not to be fucked with and to be avoided at all costs.

I had more than enough exposure that morning and just wanted to get this weed that was fucking separated into gram baggies away from my person. The thought of Thai prison and exactly how fucking stupid I was being at the time hit hard and I had to have the taxi drive pull over on the tollway so I could vomit.

Avoiding a close-call death sentence mixed with a hard hangover due to not drinking for months made me nauseous as fuck, go figure? Finally I made it to Shake's office. I stumbled out of the taxi, thanking all the gods and devils for letting me arrive. Rolled in, said hello to some old co-workers, dropped Shake's anti-Christ-arrest-me bag of shitty weed (full of stems n seeds) off. If I had been done up on trafficking for such shitty weed that woulda made it so much worse. Picture Mexican brick weed. Leave that shit in a dusty basement for a year and you're now close to what is sold in Thailand.

Said goodbye to Shake and headed to his house to pick up my turntables. His wife was home. The girlfriend who saved Shake from the machete-wielding taxi driver has now made Shake a husband. They have been living in Rangsit for the past year and she seemed to enjoy it. We chatted for a bit and I grabbed the turntables and called a taxi back to Bangkok. The shaking from the morning's misadventure had worn off and I was ready to get good sleep then hit more drink. Made it back to the hotel, carried the turntables up and slept till about 7 pm. Had literally enough excitement and partying the past twenty-four hours that I didn't need to go back out. But I did :)

DJing on the weekend

That night I played a show at an art gallery in Bangkok where I used to have a monthly gig at. Did an all-vinyl set, which was great. It's not so common these days to use only vinyl when DJing. Got to see some old friends and rap about the craziness that was KSA. Happy times. My alcohol tolerance not so happy. After my set was finished I took a taxi back to my hotel but I couldn't remember which side of the street it was on. After walking back and forth about twenty times for an hour I finally found it. I had about three hours until I had to leave for my flight. I crashed hard instantly. The loudest motherfucking alarm then went off in what seemed like four minutes.

Going back to Saudi

I was not sure I would even be allowed to bring the turntables back into the country. While I was in KSA music was forbidden and not heard anywhere Sharia law forbids music and all music is haram. At the time writing this there have been some small progressive changes. The past year there have now been a few concerts in Saudi Arabia's "liberal city", Jeddah. There was no music allowed in public in my time. Malls, restaurants, etc. None of them had music playing in them. This was actually a nice change compared to Thailand's ever-present top ten songs on repeat, for fifteen years in a row, at any indoor shopping facility. If I have to hear "Tonight" or "Call me Maybe" again in my life I'll kick a puppy in its face. So, fingers crossed, shower, turntables, passport, taxi, airport, flight, fuck me, back in KSA. Sigh … my first day back I went off on a cadet for cheating during his test. He started to eat his notebook paper with a sad look on his face as I yelled at him. He was 23 years old. What the fuck am I doing here?

Homebrew: Let's make shitty wine

The group of co-workers whom I hung out with usually comprised the Viking, the Small Scotsman, Potter, one South African and Jersey. We all lived in the same building except for Jersey who was now in a trailer park forty minutes north of us. One night, in what must have been early December, we walked to a local Indian restaurant. On the way home, Gary the South African turned to us and asked if we were drinking with him that weekend. My ears perked up and I smiled. "Happy to join."

That weekend we went to Gary's apartment to sample his homemade wine. The only alcohol available to us was a moonshine made by locals called "al-raq". It tasted like spoiled gasoline and was awful. People died from drinking it. Homemade wine was highly preferred. Gary had been perfecting his wine-making skills over several months. He stored it in large glass bottles that the shitty grape juice came in. Potter would smuggle back in wine yeast and Gary would brew using large water deposit bottles in a standing closet in his bedroom. The wine itself did the job ok but it needed mixing with 7-Up. It certainly got you semi-drunk-like. We finished off about four bottles between the five of us and traded YouTube turns with stand-up comedians. FYI the Small Scotsman had the worst taste in stand-up.

The next few weeks Gary had me over to his apartment to teach me his trade. Back in South Africa, Gary brewed legit booze while at college. Proper bottles and all. Here in KSA he was left with a MacGyver-style type of brewing. We went to Panda shopping mart to load up on juice. This particular week we went with Ceres juice. It doesn't really matter what juice you use but from years of experience in the homebrew life, the less sugar the better. And if it does have sugar, it is preferable that it is natural. Back at Gary's we opened all the juices and dumped them in a water-deposit bottle. Added yeast and more sugar. Closed. Turned the bottle upside-down several times so the yeast mixed. Peirced top of lid. Threw in standing closet (a wardrobe for my British readers). Let sit for three weeks-ish.

Glen was ready to rack a current batch that had been brewing. Racking is when you filter the wine and let it sit for a couple more days. Perhaps this isn't the official method of wine racking but it is the KSA method, so leave the comments on Amazon if you must. The more you rack the better the wine will be and the longer you let it brew, the better it will taste, fine wine and age and whatnot.

Here is what NOT to do if you ever find yourself home brewing. Gary would take a fishing hose and put it in the brewing wine then with his mouth siphon it out into another bottle. This mouth bacteria taints the taste and contaminates the batch. A more experienced brewer in KSA later schooled me. He'll be introduced in a couple chapters. For the time being with Gary's wine we would now all have some semi-ok South African mouth-tainted wine for Christmas.

Rymus

One of the greatest things about living abroad is seeing and experiencing new holidays you never knew existed, like Song Kran in Thailand, Obon festival of souls in Japan and Carnival in Brazil. Holidays being haram in KSA you had to make up your own. One such made-up holiday in KSA was Rymus. Rymus was a combination of Christmas and a co-worker Ryan's birthday, celebrated annually in Bahrain. The Viking approached me one day in early December and said, "Jersey already knows but you are invited to Rymus this weekend in Bahrain, come, you will enjoy it I promise."

Gary, Potter, the Viking, the Small Scotsman, Paul, an older Englishman, and I waited outside our apartment building for our driver, Waseem. Waseem was a Pakistani who ran a private car company. We used him and his brothers all the time. Airports, Bahrain runs, hospital trips, you name it. The driving in Saudi is the worst in the world. You WILL see an accident once a week, at least. So having a reliable safe driver is of utmost importance.

Causeway

Waseem arrived in his ten-seat SUV. We hopped in and headed to the causeway. The causeway is an eleven-mile bridge that connects KSA to Bahrain. It could take us one hour or seven hours to cross. Every weekend the entire population of the Eastern province headed over the causeway to indulge in a variety of haram activities available in Bahrain. Bahrain is an Islamic country however they are much more relaxed than their older brother KSA. In Bahrain women can drive, you can buy alcohol, pork, go clubbing, talk to women, celebrate non Islamic holidays, see live music and movies, and several other normal activities that you are deprived of while living in KSA.

The causeway first had a toll then we drove about four miles to the immigration area. Here is where we saw the absolute worst of the worst drivers. Imagine 2,000 cars coming from a two-lane highway to ten immigration lines. It's as beautiful as it sounds. Our car would approach the KSA immigration first. IDs and passports were handed over through the window to a Saudi immigration officer. IDs and passports were stamped and checked. We then went to what is known as "no-man's land". No-man's-land is not KSA and it's not Bahrain. Neither country holds power in this stretch of the bridge. This no-man's-land lasts until Bahrain immigration. We then approached another toll window for Bahrain immigration and repeated the same process. IDs and passports were checked and stamped. Finally we approached Bahrain customs. Since there was literally nothing anyone would or could smuggle out of KSA, the customs into Bahrain on the causeway was always quick and easy. An officer would peek in our car's window (maybe), nod then wave us through. In over 130 trips to Bahrain not once did I see a customs agent open up a car when entering Bahrain.

Arrival in Bahrain

Manama is kind of a financial district with lots of hotels for people coming over from KSA and a couple malls. That's about it. It is a place for Devil's wishlisting when living in KSA. The first place we would go to when arriving in Bahrain was a bottle shop. A bottle shop is a booze store. There were three in the capital of Bahrain, Manama. A funny law concerning booze shops in Bahrain stated that no national garb could be worn while inside the shops. Saudis buying booze couldn't wear their thobes. In the parking lot of each shop we saw all the Saudis changing out of their thobes usually into gym clothes, so they could go inside and buy alcohol.

The shops were fairly big. They had a large cold-single-bottle area, cases of beer, wine and liquor. We all got our own poison for the weekend. The next stop was the pork store. Back then Manama had two grocers that sold pork. Each grocer had a small room separate from the rest of the store that only sold pork products. Our usual pick was Al-Jazeera. The grocery shopping in KSA was so fucking dismal that I found myself coming to Bahrain just to shop at Al Jazeera market.

The entire lot of us loaded up on every single type of pork product you could imagine: bacon, maple bacon, apple-smoked bacon, salami, peperoni, back bacon, ham, honey ham, sausages, etc. It was heaven.

The hotel of haram

Our hotel for the weekend was a duplex inside a large hotel called Elite-5. It had four bedrooms and three bathrooms, a kitchen, a large living room and one stairwell. It took us about twenty minutes to unload all the alcohol and pork and there was too much to fit in the refrigerator and freezer. We had to start cooking full packets of bacon to make room in the fridge for the rest of our pork haul.

I never knew how much I missed bacon until I couldn't eat it for several months. It was probably around 4 pm by now and we all were drinking heavy and fast. This weekend was Bahrain's Independence Day, don't ask what their independence day was from, 'cos I never found out. The Bahrainis were all out driving around in their cars and waving flags. They seemed friendly enough and more approachable than the Saudis.

Match point

There was only one venue the crew planned to visit that evening. The famous Match Point "sports bar" at the bottom of Ramee palace hotel. The sign said sports bar but in reality it was a hooker bar with some pool tables. The part of town we were in was near America's 5th naval fleet. Gotta keep Iran on its toes. Needless to say, where there are army bases there are bars. And these bars had what is known in Bahrain as "friends of the causeway" aka hookers. The majority of the hookers were from China and Thailand.

The fellas had all been there several times before and I was happy just to be drinking with a belly full of pork and to be able to see and talk to women. Around 9 pm we left the hotel on foot. Potter had been downing gin and tonics all day and could barely walk. We had about a fourteen-minute walk to Match Point and about halfway Potter fell into a ditch so we carried him the remainder. I was not confident that we could get him into the bar – in any western country he would have never been allowed inside. His legs were absolutely limp and he could barely speak. I was assured two things by the group: 1. He would 100% get into Match Point and 2. Potter would be drinking again upright within an hour.

The entrance to Match Point could be reached by walking behind the Ramee Palace Hotel and cutting through a parking lot.

Once inside the stagnant stench of cigarettes and cheap perfume were unmistakably filtered throughout your airways with every breath. The music was the usual shitty club music. The patrons were a mix of foreigners working in Saudi, older Saudi men and Thai working girls.

They had Corona so I was happy. Any beer would have been fine though. We threw Potter in a corner and commenced more excessive drinking for several hours. Potter did indeed awaken with a second wind. I felt a tap on my shoulder and it was Potter, drink in hand and happier than when Gryffindor won the quidditch tournament in *The Philosopher's Stone*. We played several games of pool, chatted with the ladies and stayed until bar close.

Next morning match point

I had the master bedroom and woke to the wonderful smell of bacon. Potter and Gary were cooking. The only one who had managed to get any action the previous evening was Potter. Gary told me at like 4 am Potter left their room, went outside for twenty minutes then came back in. Potter had lucked out on one of his "samesies" apps and went out in the middle of the night to give some lucky Bahraini a hand-job in his car. Well, at least someone got to get some ass I suppose. Rymus was a success. Morning drinking and a half-day of bacon took up the remainder of what little time we had left. Waseem picked us up and we make the dreaded journey back to 18th Street in Dammam. The only thing worse than living in KSA is driving back on that fucking causeway semi-drunk and dealing with 2,000 other cars filled with Saudis who are also drunk and still can't drive worth their country's weight in sand. The drive back from Bahrain could be one hour or eight hours. That particular day it was an average three-hour return. Not terrible.

The convert

Several months in, there arrived a new teacher. We called him Becky. Becky was a special type of curtain laced ass bitch. Becky was the youngest ever to come to this programme. He was in his mid-20s, bald, had no experience of the Middle East, and had only worked as an elementary afterschool programme teacher in South Korea. He was now working with old angry adult men, and extremely malevolent Saudi cadets his own age. To make matters worse he was a convert.

Converts are westerners that convert to Islam whilst in KSA or shortly before coming to KSA. They were annoying as fuck (mostly). How could you tell if someone was a convert? Don't worry, they'd tell you. They were the vegans of the white Middle

Eastern expats. Becky's favourite daily activity would be to sit in the break rooms and unwrap his holy Quran so that everyone would see. He insisted on going to every prayer while at work. On top of this, Becky would try and peacock with the other teachers because he was inexperienced, new, part Asperger and so deep in the closet he was finding Christmas presents.

His favourite foe to try and peacock with was Florida. For whatever reason, he hated Florida. Florida as you know by now wasn't the best self-editing man to walk the earth. It is possible Florida talked some shit on Islam around Becky. Still don't know why. Needless to say Becky was a special type of regularly butt-hurt bitch. One day in the van Florida and Becky finally made love. By made love I mean they finally erupted. Becky was going in on Florida for something that was most likely deserved but Florida had had enough and went off on him. "You're an androgynous bitch with man boobs!" Oh, I mustn't forget, Becky, he looked like a reject from an Aphex Twin video. Don't know Aphex Twin? Go watch "Come to Daddy" or "Window Licker" and you'll get the picture. Florida's accurate burn on Becky in front of everyone must have really sanded up Becky's vagina because the next day Becky turned in his thirty-day notice. Unfortunately for us all he later decided to stay.

First time back to western culture: DC trip

Every January our company would send us back to D.C. to get our KSA visas processed in the Watergate building. It was a paid excursion with a per diem, which was nice. It was a week out of KSA and in a country with actual freedom. The first thing I noticed when landing was: wow, no wonder some many terrorist organizations hate us, everything here is forbidden and haram. I sat in an airport bar drinking alcohol during prayer time while my female server brought me more alcohol and a female in a tank top sat next to me. None of those things are accepted in KSA. It was a bit of a smack in the face having been locked away with no public advertisements, no pictures of people, no art, no music and no public communication.

I started to imagine what an American would do if they knew of a culture where all the things not deemed appropriate or accepted by American standards were going on in another hypothetical country. The most heinous of crimes in KSA is the renouncement of God, with homosexuality coming in at a close second. Both legal in USA. What are some of the worst things people do that we as Americans do not tolerate? Child rape comes to mind. What if you knew of a country where child rape was normal? You would probably want to fuck with them as well, right? Please do not get it twisted, I am not comparing child rape to atheism or samesies. I am drawing what two different cultures consider to be extreme no-nos.

Music video

While back in the States, I took advantage of every second I had and filmed a music video in my hometown of Pittsburgh. In addition to consulting for foreign military governments I spent my time outside of work doing various music endeavours. Music is a great part of my life but the health insurance sucks. A rapper I was working with drove in and we filmed a video for a song we did at a local record shop. I was able to get several friends in the video and even some old co-workers from Thailand, who were now living in Pittsburgh. Great times. After seeing the family for a couple days it was back to DC to scoop up the passport then back to KSA.

Friends of the causeway

On a weekend in Bahrain, while on the drink, Potter, Jersey and the Small Scotsman were in our usual digs. Cooking up some bacon. The Scotsman left for the afternoon to go see some probably shitty movie with a lady friend. He returned after and told us some disturbing news. The girl he went to the movies with was a Thai chef at one of the many Thai restaurants in Bahrain. There was a large Thai community there. There were about six or more Thai restaurants in the capital of Manama, probably eight Thai massage shops, I assume the happy ending type, and probably several hundred working girls. With a combination of the air force base, KSA foreign workers and horny Saudis there was a high demand for pay-to-play adult activities.

The Scotsman's date told him how she had been helping a girl who was taken out of a bar she worked at by a Bahraini, who told her they would go to a beach to relax but in fact had a group of guys waiting at the beach and they all gang-raped her. It got worse, this fucker took her wallet AND passport and dumped her in the street. Fucking men. Brutal.

Felt absolutely terrible for this poor girl. Having spent five years plus in Thailand I got a lotta love and respect for the Thais. This girl was just trying to make a living and send money back to her family, probably taking care of a child whose dad had run off. She came to Bahrain to rack up loot and got this done to her? Absolutely disgusting.

We did our usual for the remainder of our time in Bahrain: bacon, beer, club, bacon. We found a restaurant in Manama that served booze during breakfast. We got absolutely lit. Waseem picked us up, we were heading back to KSA on the causeway, and my stomach was not doing well. I was gonna throw up. Jersey said, "We can stop buddy, don't try to hold it in, we'll stop for you." At no-man's-land there was a bathroom, I thought I could hold it in until there.

Fortunately enough I could. I ran out the car and barely made it. Projectile vomitted everywhere in the stall. About three solid minutes of Russian-spaceship-bacon-vodka sprayed out like a ticket machine at Chuckie cheese.

I got back in the car and collected myself. Jersey explained he hoped we could have stopped on the bridge portion over the water so he could have filmed me vomiting from the bridge. Thanks, Jersey.

Dangling vacations

You got dank vacations when working in KSA. However you were always at the mercy of whatever military outfit you found yourself working for. The cadets would get four months plus of vacation per year. We would get about 50-65% of that if we were lucky. We would always have to wait until the day before to be told if we were to come in and sit or if we were granted leave. Order of usual events went like this: the Captain went to our British supervisor first, then said we could have the week off. Then he went to our company's direct supervisor. They both went round the break rooms and informed us that we had the week off and should book plane tickets. KSA is so awful you always,

always, always leave whenever possible. When announced we all immediately booked tickets. This particular time all went well. We were all granted a week's worth of leave. Most of my friends were going to Thailand, Koh samui. Beaches, cheap beer, beautiful girls everywhere.

Having lived in Thailand since '07 and finding myself with the financial means to travel really anywhere I wanted to, I decided I would go to Egypt. Egypt had beaches, pyramids and a couple of second-hand shops with vinyl records. I had been researching prior to the eagerly awaited possible announcement of said week off. I had even managed to secure a DJ gig at a club in Egypt. Yes!!! Record shopping, pyramids, DJing, beach. Life. Winning.

We were all on our phones the entire van ride home booking hotels. The driver got a call as we were pulling on to 18th Street. It was our company's supervisor. The Captain said we had to go into work the following day otherwise we couldn't take the week off. Sadism at its finest. The Captain knew we had all booked trips as soon as we found out at work. Well if I had grown up molesting my female relatives then I suppose I might have become as sadistic as this guy.

It didn't bother me too much as I hadn't booked my plane ticket yet. I had no Internet data on my phone so I always waited to go home to book. Several teachers had already booked though. Lots of doors were slammed and things thrown but what are you going do? Quit? None of this time off was in our contracts so there was nothing to be upset about. However, they had been going through this bullshit with the air force for years and it would indeed try you after the fifth time.

I booked my ticket, Bahrain to Cairo round trip. The next day I and a co-worker, Isiah, who I had worked with in Thailand, both hopped in a taxi to go to Bahrain and fly out. I tired talking Isaiah into going to Egypt but he missed his Thai girlfriend and was a lil sketched out about Egypt. My supervisor begged me not to go to Egypt. He said it wasn't safe for Americans there, certainly not white Americans. But my beard was looking good and with sunglasses on I was able to pass for Syrian most of the time. The Arabic I could speak, I spoke well. Wasn't worried and was young at the time. Gotta have a little bit of danger if you're ever gonna get to Thompson's place of definitions.

Night before flight to Egypt

So, Isaiah and I arrive in Bahrain. We both have early morning flights, like 4 am and 6 am. We hit the clubs. We were sauced up and I saw one of my Bahrain crushes dancing, this short-haired Filipina who worked as a receptionist at one of the hotels we would regularly stay at. I always flirted with her when we stayed there but never asked her out. She looked like Posh Spice and I had been crushing on her heavy since the first time I saw her. She would always send fruit baskets to my room. I was finally able to get one of her friends to introduce me to her that night and we hit if off quite well. We had both lived in Japan several years back and I grew up studying Filipino martial arts so we had plenty to talk about.

We were at the bar of the club and I was making her laugh. We talked about my time in Japan and how miserable it was living in the Middle East. I told her I had beers back at my hotel. She, Isaiah and I headed back to our hotel. Isaiah was bombed and tired, we had been at work all day, not working but still up at 6 am nonetheless. So Isaiah crashed. Posh and I headed back to my room. We made out and she asked if I had a condom. I am rock hard. One, I haven't had sex in about five months and two, I'm about to have sex with Filipino POSH SPICE! Fuck me. No, I do not have a condom. Why would I have a condom? I never got laid or had sex there. Wasn't expecting to get laid that night, nor get laid in Egypt. So I ran outside to the nearest gas station, bought condoms and ran back.

I had about thirty minutes before I need to leave for the airport. We were kissing in bed and she took my pants down and starting blowing me. She grabbed my dick and said let's fuck. I told her I had to leave for the airport in ten minutes, I'm not sure if we had enough time. She rolled her eyes and said, "Fuck my ass, you'll come fast." Dear diary, jack................pot. Posh was right. Gave her a hug goodbye as I got in my taxi. Vacation off to a good start.

I headed to the Bahrain airport. You couldn't check in for flights in Bahrain until three hours before the departure time. Wanna know why? Because foreigners get faded-ass drunk inside and miss their flight and cause a ruckus.

Egypt

The plane landed in Cairo and I immediately noticed the dry old smell inside of the airport. This airport was old as shit and looked like it hadn't been dusted since Nixon was in office. Strangely enough Egypt had visa on arrival for many nationalities. Americans were on the V.O.A. list too. This meant no visa or passport arrangement prior to flying.

All I had booked at this time was a hotel in Cairo, DJ gig and a ticket back to KSA. That's it. I walked out of the airport and there were 300 Egyptian taxi drivers all yelling at me. "My friend, my friend, what hotel? Pyramids? Nile? Come to my car, I take you, this way." I chose one, got in the taxi and showed him my hotel address.

The city of Cairo looked old and run down. With crack-stacks of little apartment units everywhere. The roads were crowded and it was dusty and muggy. There weren't any camels walking around. Just old, unkempt buildings and cars. A mosque thrown in here and there. We finally arrived at the hotel and I checked in. It was about $30 a night, had a hot shower and a bar on the roof. I don't remember why I picked this hotel as it was pretty far away from the pyramids. I think I picked it 'cos it was close to the DJ gig and the record stores I planned on going to. The pyramids aren't even in Cairo. They're in Giza, which is a different city entirely. Not too far away but far enough. I dropped my bags off in my room and headed up to the restaurant on the roof where you could order beer. I had two Egyptian beers and looked at the skyline of the city. Pretty surreal being in Egypt drinking beer. It had been a long 24 hours.

First morning in Egypt

The following morning I awoke to a dying, almost-empty battery on my cell phone. Then I noticed the outlets wouldn't work with my charger. I needed to find a charger quickly as Egypt needed photos and an 80s baby like me wanted his phone charged and ready.

I walked down to reception and asked where I could buy a charger or adapter and I was given really shitty directions. One thing I absolutely hate is people who can't give good directions. It's a huge tell of mental ability and character. I just nodded and left to try and find it on my own.

Enter Hamid

I walked outside, turned right and didn't even get two blocks when a man a little older than me approached. "Hey boss, how are you? Is it your first time in Egypt?" he asked. My this-man-is-going-rob-me alarm bells started ringing. I said yes and kept walking. He walked next to me continuing the conversation. Egyptians not only have a golden tongue but can and will talk endlessly for days. He said that I walked like an Egyptian, "slowly". Asked if I spoke Arabic. I said a little. He said, "Let me teach you some Arabic, my friend. You know what happens if you stick your fingers in an outlet?"

"You die?" I responded.

"You get shocked and you run away; in Arabic we say shook-run for thank you".

Dear reader, it sounds similar but it's more of a "shu-kraahn" pronunciation. I laughed and he asked me where I was going. I explained I was trying to find a store to buy a charger for my phone. He said, "Oh, my friend, I know where it is, please come with me I'll take you there." Now I was like ok word, 'cos I wasn't gonna walk around all day looking for this charger. My new friend's name was Hamid. He and his family ran a tour agency on this road that had been in his family for generations.

We reached the store and he showed me where the charges were. We headed back to my hotel and he said that if I needed any help while in Cairo he would be happy to arrange anything for me. I said I actually needed lots of shit planned. I had lots I needed to do and none of it was organized or booked. He invited me in to his shop for tea. The first thing he did was bring me tea and then he handed me a book. He instructed me to open the book and read any of the pages. He insisted I read some of these pages before we talked business. The book was a homemade scrapbook of hand-written reviews and recommendations from previous tourists and foreigners that used his services. I was impressed and had confidence I could book anything with him and he wouldn't bend me over too far on the price.

He said he wanted me to be assured he was a solid tour agency and would only provide me with the best of services. I said cools and we started picking ish out. First, the pyramids, I need to do the pyramids, Hamid. Picked out a couple of other notable ancient Egyptian sites as well. I also wanted to do a cruise on the Nile. I also had these seven shops I needed to go to. He looked at the list of shops and was like, "Why on earth do you want to go to these places? What are they? How do you know about them?"

Buying records abroad

Vinyl did not survive in the Middle East. When you tell people you collect and play vinyl records they are puzzled as hell. Luckily I learned how to say in Arabic: "I am looking for second hand vinyl records." Hamid laughed and said ok. Some of these addresses were not businesses but people's houses. I said I needed to go there, and asked if he could call and make appointments as well as arrange transportation. He explained this couldn't all happen in a day. I split it up throughout the week. Hamid was essential in my vinyl missions. The pyramids and tourist shit on day one and two and the records after that. Word.

My driver

Hamid called up his sidekick Mr. Zoohaire, who was to be my private driver for the week. Zoohaire arrived ten minutes later and we were off to the pyramids. The drive was about an hour west of Cairo. Zoohaire was driving an old Camry and he was about 65 years old. Didn't speak much English so we pigeon talked the entire day. Pigeon talk, sometimes referred to as pigeon English, is very basic unconjugated English. Instead of how are you, you say "you good?", "where you from?" Kinda like caveman talk. The smaller and simpler the words are, the more conversation you can have. My Arabic was not as good as his English so we kept it in English the majority of the day.

Pyramids

As we drove through Cairo, over the Nile, I got a sense of history and what could only be described as a historical wowness. This place was old as fuck. It's in the bible old. AND it's Indiana jones' first movie :) We arrived in Giza. We pulled up to a small divided road and I could see the pyramids in the distance. Zoohaire directed me into a small tea shop. I entered and several Egyptian men came up to me with books. They explained I could see the pyramids by horse, camel or carriage. I realized Hamid's daily fee was only for the driver at this time. I wasn't about to argue with my driver about having to pay again once there. Not his farm and not his pig. I wanted to see the pyramids and I wasn't about to let another $20 fuck it up. I asked them which was better, camel or horse? They explained that the camel dips when it walks so a horse would be easier on the thighs.

A horse it was. We (my new guide and I) had about a two-mile walk up to the actual pyramids themselves but first we went to a lookout point for pictures. We were still on this small road that lead to the sandy desert part when I asked if we can bring beer. The guide laughed and said, "Yes, of course." Now I was happy as shit. Drinking beer at the pyramids. Fuck yea. Sadly this was never going to happen. We got to the end of the road and he put up his hands and said, "Oops, no beer." I didn't pay any mind 'cos this was still cool as shit. I began to feel that riding this horse was quite bumpy. Every time the horse stepped my body bounced up at least an inch off the saddle and came back down, smack. After about ten minutes my balls were not into this at all. It got to be so painful that I said fuck the horse and walked.

We got to a lookout where guides have tourists pose with the pyramids in the background with their hands up and it looks like you're pinching the tip of the pyramids. Very touristy but a great shot and a great view of the pyramids.

On our way down from this lookout point I noticed that there was an excavation site at the base of the sphinx. My guide went on to explain that excavating never stops in Giza. They are constantly finding new sites and new artefacts, new buried rooms and tombs. I could spend months here, I thought to myself. All that history still being surfaced. Amazing.

The guide asked me if I wanted to go into the excavations. Of course I wanted to go into the excavations. He said he would take me but I COULD NOT take any pictures or we would both be in serious trouble. "Why?" I ask. He said no one was supposed to go in except the archaeologists because they were all new digs. I promised not to take photos and he nodded.

The first dig we approached looked like a square hole in the ground with old stone steps going down at a 45-degree angle. He looked around real quick and palmed one of the workers inside some money and said, "Ok, go go go, remember no picture!" I scrambled down the steps and entered a large room. There were three workers dusting off old hieroglyphics.

Hieroglyphics are pretty funny to look at. Their colour has strangely enough not faded over what, 4,500 years? This particular wall had people milking some type of cow or farm animal and collecting its milk and drinking it. They looked kinda drunk. Did Egyptians ferment milk? The workers then pointed me to a small opening in the back of the room that lead down a small unlit hallway and a larger room. They gave me a flashlight and I headed down. At this point I felt totally like Indiana Jones. My steps stuttered as I thought about booby-traps, lol. I entered a massive room with a huge jet-black stone sarcophagus. The Egyptians working in this site spoke little English. Was quite a feeling standing inside a room that was thousands of years old that virtually no one else had been in since it was in use. The Japanese would call this Tamashi-i, a Shinto phrase used to describe the accumulated spirit of a particularly awe-inspiring place.

Aside from checking out the walls with hieroglyphics there's not too much else to do in these ruins / burial chambers so I headed out and thanked them for letting me come down in and explore.

We hit several other "no tourist sites" then did the big boys. There are three pyramids in Giza. They aren't nearly as big as you might think. You can scale the largest one in about eleven minutes, I reckon. You are NOT supposed to walk on or climb them but of course several people do. I was not one of them.

After the pyramids we walked down to the sphinx and took

some pictures. The sphinx is missing its nose because people used it for target practice back in the day. My friend's father is Egyptian. He would tell us stories about him in his high-school days going to party at the sphinx and climbing all over it. Nothing was regulated at the time. Now it was very different. Measures had been put in place to help preserve these sites.

My driver and I hit up a couple more spots around Giza then I returned to the hotel for a nap. That night I had a cruise on the river Nile.

The Nile cruise

This time Hamid drove me to the docking port. It was only about twelve blocks from my hotel. He instructed me I could walk back and would be safe but to not under any circumstances stop and talk to anyone. He reiterated this several times, which led me to believe it might not be as safe as he said it would be. The cruise was fine. It was a double-decker boat that could hold about two hundred people. I was the only westerner on board. They started out the cruise with some traditional Egyptian dancing with these long sticks that the dancers (male) would slap onto the ground. It was some of the dankest music I've ever heard. These male dancers were followed up by traditional Egyptian belly dancing. The woman, Egyptian of course, came out in amongst the crowd and belly-danced with two silk scarves in her hands that she draped around various men's necks.

The others on this boat were all Arabs. Lots of families. Watching the Arab husbands watching this belly dancer was probably the happiest I've ever seen an Arab. Their arms were up snapping and clapping to the music. They all took pics of their sons with the belly dancer draping her arms around their precious little princes. This entire time their wives were covered head to toe in their burkas. 70% with only their eyes visible. None of them with hair out.

Wonder what's going through their head at this moment? My husband is gawking at a practically naked woman while she gyrates sexual movements towards him. He smiles and loves it.

Dear reader, keep in mind that the burka is a cultural garment. There are Christian women in the Middle East who cover their hair and heads daily. Some wear burkas too. One convert explained it to me like this. Arab men think of their women like a child thinks of a candy bar. Why would you walk around with a candy bar unopen, out of its wrapper? Same thing. Women not being candy, not sure how they arrived at this mentality but now you get it.

Cruise ended. Walked home quite safely with no problems. On a bridge I took back to my hotel there were three musicians. I stopped briefly, smiled and nodded to their music and kept walking. This was immediately met with angry screams and gestures of shock and offense because I didn't put any money in their hat. A ten-second stop, a smile and a nod did not merit a donation. Fuck that.

DJing in Cairo

The following day was my DJ gig and rest was needed. I woke up late and Hamid took me to lunch. We ate a traditional spicy cold noodle dish that consisted of macaroni, spices, peas and tomatoes. After lunch Hamid arranged for my driver to take me to the club that evening. At about 7 pm I packed up my DJ bag (seratto, laptop, vinyl) and headed to Hamid's shop. Hamid explained my usual driver was sick so he had found me another one. An old white Corolla rolled up and the driver got out. He was an older Egyptian man, about six foot two, slender, dark, moustache and an eye patch. He had the look of a Bond villain, a villain that wasn't casted because of his deep kidnap-you-and-never-see-the-light-of-day-no-quarter vibe. I still kick myself for not getting a picture with this guy.

We set off to find the club. I knocked on the door of what I thought was the venue but no one answered. It was just a black wall with a metal door. No sign. The driver said this was it. I decided that this couldn't be a music venue. So we went next door. We walked inside and it was a darkly lit red room with about six tables and a stage. There was a belly dancer on stage with a man doing karaoke and about seven old Egyptian guys sitting at a table watching them. As soon as I entered the music stopped and they all stared at me. "Fuck, don't let this be the venue. Pllllleeeeeeease don't let this be the venue."

I had booked the show via a promoter on Facebook. It was at a music venue that does indie art shows. Saw pics from past events and it looked like a solid spot and crowd. This was not that. My driver talked to them and they pointed back towards where we came from. The Bond villain and I walked back outside and noticed an alleyway between the two buildings. Bond villain said we should go down the alley, maybe there would be a back door. We started to walk down and I noticed how deep and long this alley was. Halfway down were two younger Egyptians in leather jackets smoking, with an unapproachable glare about them. They said they would take us to the venue. The driver didn't know the name of the place and I hadn't told them. What was about to happen? I was thinking this is it. All my gear is about to get jacked. This sucks. I walked down a back alley in Cairo with $3,000 worth of gear on my back. They motioned for us to go deeper down the alley. Reluctantly I followed. We reached the end of the alley and there was a locked door. They pounded on it but no one answered. I was fairly confident nothing good was going to come of me being at the end of this no-exit-alley with these three guys so I said I would try the street door again. I quickly headed out the alley and hit the street. Finally, street lights and unconfined space. I went back to the original door and started banging loudly. We could now hear music inside. Finally they opened it up and welcomed me. The club hadn't opened yet. I went to the sound guy. Told him I was using vinyl and we needed to set up turntables. A half hour later the gear was set up and the sound check was a smooth yes. I've done over 1,000 sound checks since I started DJing and the last place I'd expect for there to be no problems was in Cairo, Egypt, with a sound guy who spoke no English. Al'humdulalah.

Customers slowly started to come in and lightly fill up the place. My selection was not their cup of tea. Prior to booking this gig I confirmed with the promoter that I play funk and soul and trip-hop with a little 90s hip-hop here and there mixed with turntablism. These genres were perfect for art-house gigs. This club was primarily used for art-house gigs on this night. An art-house gig is when DJs are hired for various venues and you aren't blasting music all night. They are primarily done with the genres mentioned above. Good drinking music. I've done hundreds, literally hundreds of arthouse gigs in Asia. This crowd wanted "smoke weed every day and drake", not James Brown and The Meters. I had some shitty music on my hard drive so ended up feeding some meat to the lions and drinking plenty of beer. I was happy to have been able to DJ in fucking Cairo, Egypt, so no harm no foul. Plus, my driver had an eye patch. What a night.

Record shopping

Next day was record shopping. Won't bore you with the details. Went to several secondhand shops and an old opera house. Egyptian vinyl is crazy hard to find. An old opera house called Sono records burned down in the 50s. The basement contained the majority of Egypt's vinyl records. A lot was lost.

Bus to Sharm El Sheikh

Time to go to the beach. Sharm El Sheikh is a lesser-known tropical beach area on the Red Sea that is between Egypt, Jordan and Israel. It looks like Hawaii. Absolutely gorgeous. You can fly or take a bus or drive or hitch. DO NOT HITCH. I am deathly afraid of flying so I went the bus route. Hamid took me to the public bus station and asked me if I was sure I wanted to take the bus. I reassured him I would be fine and proceeded to book a ticket. It's about eight hours or so with no stops. I had two bottles of wine, some Valium and some cheese. Everything you needed on a bus ride through Sinai, Egypt. I was good to go. I booked a one-way ticket to Sharm El Sheikh from a lovely young Egyptian girl at the counter. Waited about twenty minutes then hopped on the bus. It was a large one-level tour-type bus. Think Greyhound. Luckily there weren't many people on the bus so I got two seats to myself. I cracked open the first bottle and started out my ride.

After a few hours it was all desert. You reached the Sinai province and it was beautiful long soft browns as far as you can imagine. There were several security stops along the way. I was the only westerner on the bus and I was a lil tipsy, so I wasn't too sure how these security stops were gonna go. Alcohol was legal but I likely shouldn't have been drinking inside the bus, oh well. Valium-power to the rescue. We stopped and everyone had to get out. I threw my wine bottle inside my hoody and left it on the bus and came out with my satchel which had my passport, wallet, cigarettes and phone. The army personnel lined us up outside the bus and brought a dog out. The dog sniffed us all and they took him away. Dogs in Egypt can't smell benzos either. Then they looked at each of our passports. The solider got to me, saw my passport and said, "Americani?"

"Iowa," (Yes, in Arabic) I reply.

He looked at me and said in English "The bus? You took the bus?" and tilted his head with a smirk.

I laughed and responded in Arabic, "I have little money." He laughed and shook his head and waved me back on to the bus.

Two security stops and four hours of empty-desert-waves later we finally arrived at a middle of nowhere bus stop for Sharm El Sheikh. It didn't look like a beach town at all. Night had fallen and there were a few of what I hoped were unmarked taxis. Let's try to not get kidnapped, I thought. Two bottles of wine and however many Valium I had eaten gave me that not-gonna-get-kidnapped courage, so I went up to one of the black sedans and asked, "Taxi?" They nodded and asked which hotel. I read off the name and away we went. Six minutes later I was at the front of my hotel but couldn't see any beach anywhere. Like none whatsoever at all. Just still empty desert.

Checked in, dropped my bags off and headed to the bar.

Let's go to the beach

The bartender told me all the hotels in Sharm El Sheikh are clifftop hotels so you take a bus down the road to your hotel's private staircase to their private beach. Pretty strange setup but ok.

Next morning I walked next door to three little shops. One was a pharmacy. "Do you have anything for sleeping?" Pharmacist tosses a box of Xanax on the counter. "I'll take four boxes, habibi". Bless every pharmacist selling benzos across the world. And bless China for making them in mass quantities. I headed to the beach and it was beautiful. Swam, drank, and then hunted some dive shops. I took a taxi into what I guess you would call Sharm El Sheikh town? There were several dive and tour agencies open.

I went into one and funnily enough it was run by two beach bums. Egyptian beach bums with dreadlocks, sandals and sleeveless tees. They both had that special kinda red in their eyes too. Rapped about diving prices for a bit and then saw they offered trips to Petra in Jordan. Fuck yes! Double full-on Indiana Jones. They said it could be done in a day from Sharm El Sheikh. I was ready to go. They asked for my passport and I showed it to them. They sighed. "Americans have to be escorted the rest of the way to the pier with police. If there are more than two Americans we have to provide protection because of the kidnappings and ISIS controlled areas." It was unfortunate but not heart breaking in the least. It wasn't meant to be, my friend, they told me.

There's a massive old church in Sinai, more specifically Mt Sinai proper. St. Catherine's Monastery. It has the world's second largest collection of oldest preserved manuscripts and codices. The Vatican taking first place. I asked if we could go do that and they both violently shook their heads. "Too dangerous, Daesh everywhere there, we can't take you there either, my friend, you don't want to go there". Daesh is the Arabic word for ISIS. So I ended up just booking some dives with them for the following day. The Red Sea is supposed to have the best diving in the world. Not all was lost.

I crossed the street to another tour agency where an old fat Egyptian man was sitting, eating dates and drinking tea. I asked about Petra, his price was outrageous. Then I asked about that monastery at the top on Mt. Sinai to see what he would say, he said no problem, what time do you want to go? I told him possibly the day after tomorrow, I would come back to check. Later that afternoon while at the beach the local guide that mans the hotel's beach came up to me and offered me several tour packages on a laminated clip board. I pointed to the church and he said, "No way brother, we'll both get killed." I explained the guy in town said he'd do it for $150. The guide shook his head and said some nasty things in Arabic that I didn't know but laughed at. He then told me whoever that guy was is an asshole and just wanted my money and that he had no value for human life. He said the exact same thing the wooks at the dive shop said. Daesh everywhere, don't go. So no church this visit.

The next day I did three dives and it was OK. Nothing too special. Andaman Sea > Red Sea.

Blackhawks and Bacon

That night was let's not get kidnapped part ... 7? Having spent about six months in KSA predominantly pork free, minus Bahrain, I needed my pork fix. You could find pork in Egypt but it wasn't easy. I searched online for British pubs and I found one on the map. I checked the menu and called to confirm it was pig pork not that beef substitute filth. Real. Dead. Pig. "I'm on my way."

Walked outside my hotel to the taxi stand / tent. Showed one of the drivers where the restaurant was on Google maps. He said "far" with intonation that smacked of this-is-gonna-cost-you.

"How much?" I asked.

"$120."

Deal. I needed my pork release on vacation. Would never do this again but wanted bacon and alcohol. So I loaded up with three tall beers and climbed in his taxi. Popped two xannies and cracked my beer. Special shout-out to all the taxi drivers who let me drink in their cabs. About an hour and twenty minutes in, it was dark as. I was like WTF is taking soooo long to get to my pork. We came up to a police checkpoint and were turned around. The driver just said "mushkoolah" (problem, in Arabic), we tried another way. It was literally pitch black out, no road lights, just desert and our car on a highway. We heard a loud sound, like a rumbling, it got closer and much louder. It started to get windy and the sand picked up and blew everywhere. We stopped the car and looked up and there were two Blackhawk helicopters circling about two hundred feet above us. I looked at the driver wide eyed and completely sober at this point, WTF bro. He said "mushkoolah" and nodded. Yeah bitch, problem. WTF.

The helicopters circled about twice then peaced out. I found out later that this was the start of the invasion and war with Yemen and the G.C.C. leaders were all meeting in Sharm El Sheikh to discuss the start of the war, hence the Blackhawks. We drove for about twenty minutes more then finally I could see the lights of a town. Who in the fuck puts a British pub out in this place? It was at least an hour and forty-five minute drive with no traffic, nowhere near Sharm El Sheikh at all.

After driving four blocks into town I saw a British flag on a sign. Success. There was one car and a camel in the parking lot. I went in, ordered two pints of Guinness and four orders of bacon. Slammed the Guinness. Guinness, bacon, Blackhawks and camels. Not a bad night. Rolled back to hotel. One more day at the beach.

One more day of relaxing in the Red Sea left. I had had enough of beach and Sinai. Would go back again I suppose. Stocked up on a couple more boxes of Xanax. Packed up my bags, had one last breakfast of beach-xannies and juice, then taxi'd to the bus station.

Had a very, very, very calm bus ride back to Cairo. Gazing out at never-ending sand dunes was like a massage for the eyes. Xanny-sand for days.

Goodbye Egypt

Hamid's driver picked me up at the bus station and brought me to my hotel. Had one last night in Egypt and I hit some more record stops. Next day I met Hamid and he took me out for lunch. He then brought me back to his shop and we said goodbyes, took pictures, etc. The driver shook my hand and hugged me. He said, "When you go back home, please tell people we are not all terrorists, Egypt is safe, it's a nice country for people to visit." He had such sadness in his eyes you could tell his ability to feed his family and others like him with a similar vocation had been really fucked because of religious extremists. I assured him I would, and I did. When back in KSA I wrote up an article for a newspaper back home that I had a column in. Unfortunately about a month later there was an incident on a plane out of Sharm El Sheikh as well as several kidnappings of tourists in Sinai. Egypt was once again a no-go for foreigners. I would still go back to Cairo to this day. A year later when things cooled down, Potter went to Egypt. I put him in contact with Hamid who booked him a trip all over the country. Another friend of mine that you'll read about later also went with his boyfriend to Cairo and Hamid happily helped them with their tour activities.

I can and do talk shit openly about Arabs and their faults and what I was exposed to in this region. Confidently I can tell you they indeed are NOT all terrorist. Most of them not at all. In three years of living in the Middle East I only heard a couple of cadets shit talk about the US government and president.

There are great places to visit here. Fox News would have you think a lot of them are filled with American-flag-burning Islamic militants that would rape their own mothers just to have a chance to throw a knife at you. This is simply not the case. The most dangerous places I've been to are Manila in the Philippines and Miami, Florida.

Go see the world. Preferably with a Xanax and a beer.

Ras Tanura bombing

Ras Tanura is a small town in Saudi Arabia north of us by about thirty minutes. There is a large Aramco site there. Aramco is an American-Saudi oil business. They run the oil in KSA. Their workers live in Ras Tanura or Al Khobar, both of which are in my province, the eastern province. Jersey lived in a trailer park in Ras Tanura. Between my city of Dammam and Ras Tanura was a heavily Shia-populated neighbourhood called Qatif. For the layman and for the sake of conversation let's say Islam is divided into primarily two factions, Sunni and Shia. Sunnis are the hardcore no music, women don't work or drive, crucify pot smokers, throw gays off rooftops ones. Shias are a bit more relaxed. Iran is Shia. KSA is Sunni. They hate each other. Absolutely hate each other. And really it's more so the Sunnis who hate the Shia.

One morning we heard reports that there was suicide bomber in Qatif right near where Jersey lived. A man wearing a suicide vest under his thobe walked into a Shia mosque and blew himself up. 40+ dead. One of Jersey's co-workers was at the mosque when it happened. He got pics and sent them to us. I will say this about the pics, seventy-two virgins looks painful.

Bombing at the grocer

Two weeks after the Ras Tanura bombing another suicide bomb went off around the corner from where we lived. This time it was across the street from our grocery store, Tamimi's. I was at the gym when I found out about it. A Saudi in the sauna asked if I had been to Tamimi's in Dammam. "Of course," I responded. He then asked if I was there this morning when the bomb went off. I had absolutely no idea of the attack at all. Left the sauna and got the Viking and the Small Scotsman to bounce so we could find out what the fuck was going on. We were literally blocks from where this happened and everyone knows if you want to find foreigners go to the gym so we decided leaving the gym as soon as possible was best.

The entire team of employees living in our building met that night and decided it wasn't safe at all for us to be living there. The only other people living in the building were KSA police. KSA police are also a regular target of terrorist groups in the kingdom. Man, people hate police everywhere. I can assure you all the police do in KSA is sit in their cars on their phones.

Gambling on targets

The staff at the air force was divided into two groups. Direct-hires who worked directly for the actual Royal Saudi Air Force and those who worked for my company, a Jordanian defence contractor. The direct-hires lived on a compound about forty minutes away. A compound is a large, guarded (sometimes well, sometimes horribly) and blocked-off living area for foreigners. It has large walls around it, roadblocks, armed guards / security. Saudis were not allowed onto compounds. They didn't want us kafirs infecting them with our crazy ways. My company's employees lived in the lovely apartment building on 18th Street. Some of the direct-hires had lived in KSA for over twenty-five years. They were there when Al-Qaeda was in its prime and they were there pre 9/11. If they offered advice about anything related to KSA you would be wise to listen.

Following this second bombing, several co-workers decided they had had enough and would leave that week. One guy left that night. The next day at work I was speaking to one of the direct-hires, who had been in the country since '96. He told me to leave or make the company move us. All the direct-hires had a running bet to see if our apartment building would be attacked or bombed. It was split down the middle, LOL. Half of them said 100% yes, the other half said no.

In that same conversation the direct-hire asked me if I knew the closed-down Panda grocery store. We drove by it every day. He explained that after it closed down it had been used as a terrorist training centre. For years. It had an obstacle course, a firing range with targets, the whole lot. They finally closed the training centre down about three months prior to my arrival. Other direct-hires confirmed this.

Let's get secure

We drafted a letter addressing our concerns. We wanted to be moved to a secure location. We wanted tinted windows on our vans. The liaison we had to our company was a Palestinian man named Aziz. Aziz was our go-to for everything outside of the air force. Visas, accommodation, pay, all these aspects his responsibility. Aziz would always hear us out but could never do nothing because his hands were tied. Arabs lie, it's not a slight against them, it's just part of the culture. The same way Americans tell you things directly, the same way Japanese people don't steal, the same way Thai people smile. High-context cultures lie to save face. Sometimes for them, sometimes for you and sometimes for both. Aziz told us we couldn't get the van windows tinted because it was illegal in KSA.

"Aziz, YOUR car windows are tinted!!! WTF."

Aziz laughed, looked at the floor and said, "I'll see what I can do."

Moving us all to a secure location would be costly and take forever, so that request was a bit of a pipedream. Instead of moving us they installed the shittiest Kmart piece-of-shit door downstairs at our entrance that a disabled sloth could have broken into. They hired a 17-year-old Yemini kid for security. The Yemini kid watched "Dragon Ball Z" all day, all night. Secure as fuck.

Marching

Every April the air force would take an entire month to have their cadets practice marching. These cadets marched every day and every afternoon. Still, they needed an entire month of marching all day every day for the graduation ceremony come May. Forbes released a world survey of most active and least active countries based upon daily steps taken. Saudi Arabia was the second least active. At the graduation, princes would come, moms and dads would come and all watch in glory (seated separately by gender of course) at their little worthless children march with the falsest, most undeserved sense of pride ever to be witnessed.

We were kafirs so rather than send us home or let us go out on vacation the air force kept us coming to the base for the entire four weeks of April. The teachers had no classes or cadets so I had no reports or meetings. We slept, read, went to the gym, etc. We were getting paid so it could have been worse. I learned the Arabic alphabet during this time with the help of an older Arab co-worker named Al-Sami. I can still say it and identify several characters but reading it is a pain. The location of where each character appears in a word changes how it's written. There are twenty-eight letters in Arabic. There are three different ways you are to write each depending if it begins a word, comes in-between other letters or ends a word. On top of that there are at least five accents that you can put on each letter that change its pronunciation.

At the end of the four weeks the cadets were gifted a week off to go home and eat kabsa. The kafirs were sometimes gifted this week off but not until the day before. The captain at the time loved fucking with us. He would come around the break rooms and ask if we were going anywhere for the week off, knowing full well he hadn't told our supervisors if we were permitted to leave yet. This question was always met with: "We haven't been told anything yet, Captain." He knew we didn't know because he hadn't allowed it yet and he knew we knew that we were waiting on him. He smiled when he asked this then reminded us that "plane ticket prices are going up soon, hope you find out soon." Fucking Saudis.

Self-medicating vs international drug trafficking

I was on the causeway with Waseem, my go-to driver, one night. I just wanted a night to myself in Bahrain with beer and music. Was gonna buy a twelve-pack and blast YouTube all night. On the first part of the causeway my phone rang, it was a Facebook call. Didn't even know I could get calls from Facebook. It was my friend Amanda, she had just left Abu Dhabi and her friend had been arrested. "What happened?" I asked.

Amanda, her sister and their friend were on their way back from Southeast Asia to USA. I had recently been giving them tips on where to go to get nitrous balloons in Phnom Pehn, so I had a vague idea of their travels. They were flying from Bangkok to Abu Dhabi to USA. Their friend had purchased some Valium in Cambodia where it is over-the-counter and was stopped at security in Abu Dhabi Airport. Amanda's sister also had Valium but only a few. Their friend had three packages. There are about twelve pills per package. This was considered a trafficable offense and not under the "personal use" number.

They let Amanda and her sister go but cuffed and took away their friend. I explained to Amanda that I lived in a different country all together and unfortunately would be of no use to her or her friend. Her friend was in jail for months. Her parents had to fly there and spend thousands of dollars on lawyers who were no help at all. She was told she'd be facing fifteen years in jail there. Game over. After making her sweat three months in jail they released her. I later found out she had three BOXES of Valium which would have been over 150 pills. They were also trying to leave the airport. This means they were going through the security into the actual country, not transiting. If you try to bring in over thirty pills of anything into the Emirates that is even remotely not over-the-counter you better have a script for that shit. This all made more sense now. Trying to go into Abu Dhabi with 100+ non-scripted pill of Valium, you're going to get arrested full stop.

Cleanliness is next to … some other country

The air force base in all its glory was filled with filthy attributes. There was rarely any running water in the staff bathrooms. The cadets' bathrooms sometimes had running water but never soap. In twenty years there had never been soap anywhere on this base. These kids were filthy. I still remember one day a student named Bendar, who was one of the best-behaved students, would blow his nose on himself. No tissue, no sleeve. He would make eye contact with me and just blow his nose. Snot dripping everywhere coupled with a dumb look on his face. I would put my arms up and be like, "Habibi, laish? Darling, why?"

Saudi is still a very in-the-family-friendly place. Inbreeding is prevalent and it shows. One of the few nice cadets I met there was married to his cousin. They had a baby. That baby would likely marry its cousin and so on and so forth. Gotta keep those tribes clean ya know. The inbreeding would be on the front page of plenty of the cadet's faces as well as other people in Saudi. Classrooms were full of facial abnormalities.

What's a VPN

Sitting in the break room one day the Small Scotsman, Potter and Gary were talking about football or some other dumb British shit and one of 'em said, "It's easy with my VPN."

"What's a VPN?" I ask.

They all look at me and slowly say, "Virtual private network." My puzzled look prompted their next question. "You don't have a VPN!!!??"

"No ..."

"How the fuck do you watch porn!!!" They are now practically standing from surprise and astonishment at this point.

I reply, "Google image search, it fucking sucks."

They were rolling on the floor laughing now. I laughed too, 'cos I was so sad my porn life was so dreadful.

The Scotsman shook his head and said, "I can giv yer some vids ya poor bastard but ye need tae get yerself a proper VPN alrite. Ya can'ta stay here witout one."

I got one. Life was better.

Slumdog tells the commander he's not gay

An ex-employee from before my time had gone through a riff with Cornell and Slumdog. To take revenge after he had parted ways from the air force he made a fake Facebook profile of Slumdog declaring his homosexuality and posting all his personal details, job phone, etc. The guy would then post outrageous gay porn on the profile. Slumdog had to go tell the commander what was going on and that it wasn't true. Twice. Rough times indeed. Surprisingly both times the commander understood and paid no mind to it. While no repercussions came to Slumdog from this, take a moment and imagine going into a Saudi commander's office and explaining to him how someone made a fake Facebook profile of you (an overtly homosexual one, with pics!!!). Slumdog had to do this twice with two different commanders. Bravo, Slumdog.

Jinn

Jinn is the Arabic word for genie. There are three types of Jinn, none of which grant wishes. The Saudis are very superstitious. They say religious, but you and I would say superstitious. They believe in magic and people have received death sentences for casting magic spells. This superstitious belief about magic is stretched throughout the Middle East. I even had conversations with converts, ones I respected and liked, about how magic is just not real. They had swallowed the Kool aid and enjoyed its taste.

At the air force, I generally worked with the three South Africans. One of them had his own room and kept to himself and the other two and I shared another office. We got along great and would spend most of the day sending memes and talking about our crazy co-workers and planning vacations. Every Thursday we would go have our meeting with the commander and give him our reports. One day whilst waiting around to leave work, Cornell said, "Like that time they did the exorcism," and rolled his eyes.

I immediately perked up and asked, "What what what, you gotta tell me this now."

Jinn or at least some jinn act like poltergeists. Apparently, they can also possess people.

Slumdog explained that one day when he was teaching, a student fell over and started screaming things in Arabic. He thought it might have been a seizure so he went to get Misfir. Misfir comes in and immediately yells at two cadets to go and get the Mutawa who come in with an Imam. They rush in and start praying over the poor cadet who clearly either had mental issues or was attempting to get out of the day's classes and work. If it was a ruse, it must have been convincing enough to bring in the Mutawa and the Imam. Slumdog was inside the entire time this was going on. Afterwards Misfir explained that they performed an exorcism to rid the cadet of the evil jinn. They also asked Slumdog not to talk about it to anyone. Guess they were worried their secret exorcism rites might get into the hands of a kafir.

Let's hold passports

KSA was notorious for the mistreatment of its imported workers. Every city was littered with poor migrant workers that did trash and clean-up duty. The Saudis showed them absolutely no resemblance of humane respect. They regularly threw things at them, yelled and demoralized them all while the workers were cleaning up their rubbish. The Saudis often took their passports upon arrival and held them hostage. There were countless stories of maids from Indonesia, Cambodia and countries in Africa having their passports taken and being forced to do labour for years. In the worst cases, they would be the house sex-slaves for fathers and sons.

We were requested to turn over our passports to our company, which half of the employees did. I refused 100%. They kept them in a safe on the air force base. If something happened and you had to leave you were not permitted onto the base unless it was during work hours. The entire thing made no sense. During my second year in KSA a new labour law came out stating all companies were required to give back passports. All foreign employees had to sign a document for the labour office stating that you were indeed in possession of your passport. The international press had just too much ammo for Saudi's continuation of foreign-worker-exploitation. This is not to say it fully stopped but it certainly got not necessarily better, but less bad.

The driving

The driving, if that is what you want to call it, in KSA was dismal at best. Watching Saudis drive made the Titanic look like a nice normal docking. If you ever lived there, you have seen an accident, 100%. Take three minutes and go and YouTube Saudi drivers. KSA has one of the world's highest accident rates as well as one of the world's highest traffic death rates. It has been reported that 23 KSA residents die every day and it has been projected that KSA will have 4 million accidents per year by 2030.

In KSA when they look at traffic lights they read them as follows: green means go, yellow means go fast! And red means maybe accident. A quick survey among friends who lived in KSA threw up these three-word description of Saudi driving:

1. "Total fucking carnage"
2. "Bat shit crazy"
3. "Mad Max … wait you said three words? Mad Max inshallah"
4. "meth-induced video game"
5. "reckless erratic danger"

Don't rob banks, rob Bahrain's lost and found

Potter lost his glasses during a weekend excursion to Bahrain.

He thought he left them in the movie theatre, so we went to the mall to hit up the lost and found. The lost and found room had a massive plastic box full of wallets, Rolexes and wads of money. No glasses for Potter but easily $40,000+ of birthed false entitled belongings.

Negotiating culture

Arab culture can be described as a negotiating culture. Allow me to explain. When shopping at a bazar or market there is always an exchange of price and haggling. Even if either party is fixed on a price there still needs to be back-n-forth. Voices and opinions are to be heard out regardless of the outcome. At the air force, if a teacher was going to punish a cadet for whatever reason, the cadet needed to be heard so he could explain. Example: Cadet Faizal arrives late, the Viking gives him a D.R. (Discipline Report), the cadet will protest. If the Viking doesn't hear him out and sends him out with the D.R. immediately the cadet will remain extra pissed at the Viking for life. Why? Because the Viking would not listen to his case. Now, if the Viking listens and still sends him out then the cadet will be far less upset about the ordeal because in his mind he was able to plead his case and attempt a negotiation. This is repeated in full force in market places and is part of daily life in the Middle East. Everything has to have a story behind the price, why it cannot be lowered or why the seller can only go down in ten riyals or why the buyer can't pay the requested price. You will never see an Arab walk up to a phone shop, ask how much and pay the asked price. Negotiating is necessary, even when from the get-go both parties are cemented in whatever the topic / price is; this has been a major factor in the downfall of Western-Arab relations in the past fifty years.

No taxes, no interest on loans

Hands up for Islamic banking and one of Sharia's better laws. There were no taxes and no interest on banking loans. All salaries in the country were tax-free. If you were American you only paid tax on anything over $100,000 at the time, and this was to the American government only. Saudis who needed loans obtained them easily. This included loans for dowries. Most Asian countries have gender reverse dowries. Afghanistan, Saudi, Thailand, Cambodia ... males pay the female's parents. In Saudi, they pay a dear amount as well. Depending whether you had a job or had a good family / tribe, you could get a loan easily. The loan would be paid back w/o interest. I use the term "paid back" loosely. They also would not put leans on your house etc. In Kuwait, they did loan forgiveness. How about that?

The Blue Diamond Affair

In the late 1980s a Thai gardener was working in the royal family's palace. Several royal jewels went missing, one of which was a fifty-carat blue diamond. All in, over twenty million dollars of jewellery. The servant smuggled them out of the palace using a vacuum cleaner and sent them back to Thailand. After fleeing KSA he was arrested in Thailand and sentenced to six years in jail, served three for confessing.

KSA sent a Saudi royal family friend and businessman Mohammad Al-Ruwaili over to Thailand to track down the jewels. He went missing and is presumed dead. The same week, three Saudi diplomats who were also sent over to investigate the jewels were murdered in Bangkok. Thailand sent back the jewels with the exception of the blue diamond. The jewels sent back turned out to be counterfeit. The real jewels turned up around the neck of some of Thailand's most well-known women on the front pages of a Thai newspapers and magazines. Eat a thousand dicks KSA! Every expat in KSA applauds Thailand for this.

Because of this snafu Saudi forbade its citizens to travel to Thailand. They still go, but if immigration sees a Thai visa or stamp in their passport then they may be investigated, fined or even jailed. Trust. They still go often.

Firefighters in Rasta Nora

A shining example of public service and its effectiveness in KSA is its fire department. It is a laugh just writing Saudi fire department. Might as well say Fukushima gardening club. Jersey worked at a massive electrical training school up north. There was a huge electrical fire on campus at a generator. The first department showed up and did what to put out the ELECTRICAL FIRE? Yup. Water.

Their surprise and look of confusion when the fire became larger after putting water on it only solidified the absolute absence of any possible strand of hope one had for this society surviving if foreigners left. They are just absolutely doomed.

Ramadan

Ramadan was the best time of the year for me in KSA. Why? Because I didn't have to be there. Foreign workers generally get about five to ten weeks off. The Saudis, and Muslims worldwide, fast during daylight hours and restrict themselves from several other normal daily activities. It was always best not to be in the country during Ramadan if you weren't Muslim. Fasting was not an optional thing during this period so if you were drinking water or chewing gum outside it was gonna be a big problem. Mutawa sees you drinking water outside during Ramadan? Jail. Best way to avoid having to go to the jail to bail your foreign workers out? Send them out of the country on vacation.

Therefore, every Ramadan, our company would buy us a round trip plane ticket anywhere we wanted to go. We were paid during this time too. Win-win. My first Ramadan I went to Myanmar, USA and Thailand. Met up with Potter and the Small Scotsman in Myanmar. I flew in from Bangkok to Mandalay. Spent a night in Mandalay and we all took a bus to Bagan. Bagan is a beautiful ancient city in the middle of Myanmar with temples scattered all over. Myanmar had recently opened up to the public and had been slowly developing its tourist industry over the past several years. Back in '07 when I lived in Phuket, going to Myanmar was not a good idea and going all the way to Bagan wasn't even an option.

Myanmar has been and in many ways still is in the clutches of arguably the world's worst Junta. Led by Than Shwe. Than Shwe ranked No. 4 on "Parade" magazine's 2009 "World's Worst Dictators" list. Systematic rape, the largest child soldier army and death squads are how you can sum up Myanmar's last sixty years give or take. The only other country America has had less to do with is North Korea. Rightfully so.

The van ride to Bagan was an eleven-hour trip in a sixteen-passenger van with everyone's luggage strapped to the roof. The road out of Mandalay was fairly normal. Billboard adverts had just taken off and the few companies that were advertising looked as if they had taken pages from Madmen. The ads looked straight out of the 1960s. The roads started to get mountainous and the views of valleys and steep mountain passes were abundant and refreshing and a lil nerve racking. About half way to Bagan, we stopped at a small side-road-style restaurant. The van was cramped and we joked about riding on the roof. In Napoleonic fashion the Small Scotsman said, "I'll do it. Yeah what's wrong with that?"

"Um, you'll die?"

"Well if I die, I die then, won't I, boys." He fuckin did it. He hopped up on the roof, sat above everyone's luggage, and nestled down in-between a couple of suitcases. His size has finally done him some good.

Bagan was great. After Bagan, we headed to Kalaw.

Kalaw

Kalaw is a small mountain-trek-hub that has a really strange vibe. It's the main starting point for everyone that does a famous trek from Kalaw to Inle Lake. The town is littered with guesthouses and medium-ish sized hotels. Sprinkled throughout the town are massive Hollywood-style opium-mansion compounds. The opium trade from Myanmar had been supplying the world with heroin up until the war in Afghanistan.

Potter and the Scotsman booked their trek so we had about two days of relaxing in town. The Scotsman and I were invited to an orphanage to teach for a day. Potter declined as he had a bottle of wine, Wi-Fi, and a mission to see what sodomy laws he could break in Kalaw. When it was time to part ways, I had a logistical nightmare of a mission getting back to Thailand.

I could take a fourteen-hour van back to Mandalay or try to access an airport on the other side of the mountains and fly up to a northern airport on the boarder of Thailand's golden triangle. There was a direct five-hour highway and bus route from Kalaw to the golden triangle but because of kidnappings in the Shan state, no one would sell a foreigner a ticket. Foreigners were still forbidden from travelling in the Shan state.

I eventually found a taxi driver that would take me to the airport near Kalaw, which was about an hour away. You could only buy tickets at the airport so it was a bit of a gamble. The drive to the airport was gorgeous. Flush green rolling mountains. The airport looked like an elementary school. It was easily the smallest airport I've ever seen. Going through security was hysterical. There was an old Burmese man waving people through a non-working metal detector with a big smile on his face.

The airport did have beer so I commenced drinking. There was one other foreigner at the airport. We locked eyes, smiled and held up our beers cheers-ing in the air. The flight was surprisingly smooth and easy. Landed in this small boarder town, found a taxi and proceeded to the border crossing. I had been drinking all morning and popping Xanax every thirty minutes or so, and by the time I crossed the border I was faded to say the least.

Once on the other side of the border there was a bus station. The plan was to go south to Chiang Mai to meet up with Isiah. All the buses to Chiang Mai were full and I was not going to spend another day in opium towns. I went to a 7-Eleven and bought two beers. Chugged them and rallied up. Went up to a taxi driver and asked how much to drive me to Chiang Mai. It was a three and a half-hour drive but I was willing to pay this person's month's salary for half-a-day's work. I needed air-conditioning and Mexican food. He did it for under 4,000 baht. That was about $120. I've taken forty-minute Uber-rides that were more expensive. The rest of Ramadan was spent relaxing in Chiang Mai and beering it up with Isiah. Good times.

Music problem

I was planning on bringing back into KSA 140 records following the Ramadan break. There were three music shops in our city in KSA, all of which would get shut down by the Mutawa every so often for selling music which was considered haram. Wasn't sure if I would be allowed to bring in the records or not but I was going to try. The records were in a large hard travel suitcase that I checked in. I got to customs and put the case on the x-ray belt and walked to the other side. The agent stopped, took my case off and motioned for me to come over and open it up.

"What's in this case?"

"Phonographee estawanat." Arabic for second-hand vinyl records.

"Open it." I opened the case and showed him the records. He asked what I needed all these records for. I told him I collected them and listened to them. He shook his head, looked at me and said, "I think you have a music problem." He then waved me to go on ahead and leave. Records through. Score.

Return from Ramadan

Upon returning from Ramadan, we had several new teachers. The Viking was gone and Gary had left us for other adventures. They were replaced by some characters from the lovely island of England. These new knuckleheads only amplified the on-going craziness that was occurring daily.

Enter Mr. Salacious Crumb

The first week we were back at work the cadets still had a week off. So break room love was rolling per usual as we sat around all day waiting for something to do. One of the newer teachers was a middle-aged man from England who now lived in Southern Thailand with his Thai wife and two children.

Ever see return of the Jedi? Do you remember the little rat creature that would sit next to Jabba the hut? That creature's name was Salacious Crumb and this guy looked like Salacious Crumb grew up and became an alcoholic. You would add more clothes to him when having to look at him. He acted and behaved like he was raised by Bigfoot and wolves. Crumb would not stop talking ... ever. Endless gabber and narration. On our second day of work, this fuck literally narrated what he saw out the window the entire ride home. "Oh look that man is taking out garbage, the light is still red, will probably change to green soon, the car in front of us is going slow, oh wait, think he had it in the wrong gear, cheeky bugger." He was sitting in the third row of the van and doing this. I literally almost got out and jumped in traffic.

Next day at work, I was walking through the hallway and I thought I heard screaming. The cadets were still gone so no NCOs should be yelling. That is weird, I thought to myself. I must be imagining it. I went to the stairwell to go downstairs and outside for a smoke, and I heard it again. "Misssteeeer Al

Saaaaaaamiiiiiiii" WTF? That's a foreigner. I ran back up and I heard more yelling coming from the bathroom. I opened the bathroom door and it was fucking Crumb.

Crumb was standing in front of the bathroom stall, pants and underwear down to his ankles, dress shirt dangling and barely covering his one-inch-killer-serpent cock, his dirty little sausage fingers and hands covered in shit, wailing about and saying: "They've got the water turned off and me hands are covered in shit, you gotta help us." This is how he lost any small semblance of respect I might have guiltily awarded him.

In Asia and the Middle East, a bum-gun is often used in toilets. It's a small hose connected to the wall with a sprayer on the end. It looks exactly what people have in their kitchen sinks to spray off dishes. Many Asian countries use this sprayer and their left hand to clean up after taking a number two. Then, if they are not savages, they use toilet paper to dry up.

Crumb had clearly dived into Asian toilet culture. I immediately closed my eyes and 180d it out of the bathroom. Astonished and disgusted I went to my locker in the smoker's room next door and got some Kleenex. As I shut my locker, it hit me that I would have to hand these tissues to him, with my hand. Fuck, I hated KSA.

I went back in and thankfully he had returned to his thrown of shame and disgust. He was now sitting back on the toilet cussing up a storm with his fucking shit-covered hands on his head and he continued swearing as it was OBVIOUSLY someone else's fault that he had shit all over his hands and not his own fault. I dropped the Kleenex in the sink, told him it was there and left.

I felt like I'd just been witness to a murder or something.

Now as I walked away from the bathroom down a hallway to a separate break room, still astonished at what had just taken place, I realised immediately that I didn't even need to tell anyone about this awful crazy incident because Crumb couldn't keep his mouth shut at all, he would tell everyone this with no shame or self-regulating manner.

Fast forward to the afternoon. I and about eight other co-workers were in the break room and Crumb came in and loudly told everyone about what happened. He then came over to me and put both his hands on my shoulders and said, "This man right here saved me, didn't he. Will never forget it, bud, you're a right lad." I cringed, twice.

Crumb exits, the break room burst out laughing and I said, "He really put his hands on me, didn't he?" The water still had not been turned on throughout the remaining hours of the day. There was a shirt for the fire.

The bellhop

Now the one thing that Crumb did well was bring over his friend the bellhop. The bellhop was an old Englishman around sixty years old who had been overseas the majority of his life. The bellhop had run a go-go bar in Pattaya and loudly asserted his many marriages to prostitutes throughout his life. We called him the bellhop because this guy had his fingers in so many pies of illegal booze operations he could get anything we wanted delivered.

Drinking

There were two types of living arrangements in KSA: compound and public. Compounds were where you found bars and alcohol (real and homebrew). In the public, where we lived, alcohol was far far far less common. Saudi nationals were not allowed onto compounds. The bellhop had the in at several different compounds in our province. Most of these were invite only. He invited me out to one and I was eternally grateful. Up until this point, the only booze we could get was Gary's homebrew. Gary had left KSA over Ramadan so we were dry as dirt.

The bellhop, Crumb and I all piled into a taxi and headed to a compound in the sister city next to ours. We arrived and entered the compound. There was an ID / passport check then you went through a security door into what was about a 400-person compound. An American, we will call SGT, ran a bar there on the weekends. He had beer on tap, homemade rum as well as red and white wine for takeaway.

He had several Ethiopian bartenders who worked in KSA as nannies. They were very attractive and kept the male customers drinking throughout the night. Booze and females. The booze was good and I ended up taking several bottles of wine back home.

Throughout the following months, the bellhop would take us to various compounds and I started to see a bit of an Ethiopian mafia running all these bars. One of them had a club inside that would be filled every weekend with Ethiopian nannies dancing. This particular bar had real booze too. The real booze was $14 a shot while the homebrew booze was $3. I stuck with the homebrew. The bartender at this spot was an old friend of the bellhop. Her name was J.D. Stood for Jack Daniels. J.D. and I hit it off quite well.

She was in her mid-30s, from Ethiopia, worked as a nanny and had hit the genetic lottery. Her curves were quite possible the best I'd ever seen in my entire life. Every weekend every single guy there would hit on her and fail miserably. One weekend she asked me to go dance with her and I said sure. I had taken a creative dance class in high school and knew how to slow dance and ballroom dance quite well. I learned in high school if you can dance well girls are more likely to fuck you. So I danced a lot. J.D. was lit with joy when I would twirl her on the dance floor and do other various spinning dance moves.

She gave me her number and said to call her so we could go out. Go out? Go out where? J.D. had the in at all the bars being run by Ethiopians in our province. All compound bars would hire Ethiopian girls to bartend for obvious reasons. Guys want to drink and will stay longer if there is a pretty face to look at. God knows we were all just looking at nothing but dick all week long.

Tinder

Tinder in KSA was awful. You had a mix of Filipinos, unhappy western females and the occasional Saudi girl who would have no pics. I knew one guy who had a successful date on Tinder in KSA. He is now married to her. Long story short I was super excited to go on a date with J.D.

That weekend she had me pick her up and we went to one of her friend's compounds. I had the bellhop meet us there later. Things had been going great until about halfway through the night when she looked me dead in the eyes and asked, "What do you think about God, you believe in God right?" Fuck me. Ethiopians are known to be hardcore Christians.

I grew up with an extremely religious Irish catholic mother

and am happy to never have fuck all to do with any religion the rest of my life. Fuck me. She's already going Jeezo on me. I gave her some line about how I didn't want to be discussing theology on our first date but that I was happy to respect her views. That was the last time I talked to J.D. As soon as a person brought religion up I vacated. Proselytizing is such a turn off for me and frankly I think it shouldn't be done in the first place.

Walken

In addition to the Bellhop and Crumb we also had another new co-worker called Walken. We called him Walken because he had something of a stutter, not really a speech impediment but more like a southern drawl with a delay. Walken had lived in KSA for years as a college scholarship advisor. He was in charge of dishing out scholarships to young male college Saudis so they could go to the States. In addition to the royal family paying for their schooling overseas each student was gifted a handsome monthly stipend of $5,000. Getting these scholarships was like winning the lottery.

Walken loved living in KSA. Why? Cos he was gayer than when gay came to gay town, that's why.

Let's see if dogs smell Xanax

Throughout the year the air force would have surprise time off, which sometimes we were allowed to take, if we could find a cheap enough ticket. Since KSA sucked, we would always bust out. I am an extremely nervous flyer as you now know. On our shorter vacations, I would usually go to Thailand and see my girlfriend at the time or see old friends. One great thing about Thailand was that Xanax used to be sold openly on the street. After a succession of prime ministers it went off street, then to O.T.C. at pharmacies. Now it isn't O.T.C. and you have to either have a pharmacist in your pocket or get a script. Luckily, my doctor in Bangkok gave me scripts. However there was a period of about one and a half years that I'd have to hunt down pharmacies all over the city to try and get Xanax so flying could be tolerable.

I had found two and would buy several months' worth from them so I would be sorted for my next few flights. The first time I went back to KSA with, I dunno, maybe about thirty to sixty pills, I didn't know what to expect. They were in packaging that said Alprazolam. I had no script. I would put them in my pocket when arriving at customs.

I figured because they were not loose in some crack baggy they'd likely not fuss too much about finding them and going down that rabbit hole would entail a lot of work. They would have to look up the name alprazolam then check it with a corresponding list to see if it was a no-no or not.

So I rolled the dice and hoped for the best. Plus, I wasn't bringing these in to party with or sell, I was legitimately self-medicating for flight-anxiety. Perhaps a couple might have been taken throughout the week at night to get some extra sleep or make those two glasses of wine feel like five :)

I made it through customs no problems. I went to the bag pick up and then I saw two police with a dog approach me. Oh shite. Well, I was about to find out pretty soon if these dogs were trained to find benzos. I looked deadpan at the luggage carousel as the bags started to move around. The police got closer and closer to me with their German shepherd. They finally reached me and walked straight past. The dog did not even look in my direction all the while having six packages of Xanax in my sweatpants' pocket.

Ok, good to know. Now I could bring back in a bunch no problemo. And I did. The benzos flowed like the Nile from then on out. Crumb was tolerable. I was sleeping great. The wine was double the potency. The Saudis seemed less cruel. I was not deathly afraid of riding in cars now either.

Samesies

Since, well, ever, homosexuality aka samesies has been illegal, forbidden and haram in KSA and has been punishable with fines, public beatings, prison time and the death penalty. I have never in my life met so many samesies than in KSA. Thailand is probably the most gay-friendly country on our planet and still there is a remarkably higher number of gay men in evidence in KSA. If you think about it, it makes sense. You're gay, you go to a country where you are only surrounded by other men all day and are forbidden to talk with the opposite sex. Literally, everywhere you go, shop, eat, exercise, etc., is 100% men. If I could live somewhere surrounded entirely by women I'd certainly try it out.

At the air force, they were about ten samesies. Walken was the loudest of them all. He would regularly tell everyone in any break room stories (when neither asked nor prompted) about how many young Saudis he would defile up in his old stomping grounds. I can only picture this fifty-year-old ginger dangling these scholarships over these young confused boys' faces. His catch phrase was "everybody plaaaaaays".

Example. Literal Example:

Walken: Hey, boys, what's up? What's up?

4 teachers and myself in the break room: Not much, what's up?

Walken: Last night some of my boys from Ha'al came to town and we got fuuuuuucked up and you know ... (eyes roll back and forth pointing upwards)

Us: That's great.

Walken: Here, look at these pics! (Stands up and shoves his phone in our faces and scrolls through pics all of which are of Saudi cocks and naked men.)

Us: Walken! Jesus Christ! Fuck outta here with all that. You know we aren't gay right? We fuck women.

Walken (swiping his hand in the air and rolling his eyes): "Oh, everybody plaaaaaysssssss."

Walken, while not generally liked by most, same as Crumb, did bring some good attributes to our programme.

The move

We were all still living on 18th Street at this time. Walken had friends living in the next city over at a hotel/apartment in Al Khobar. Walken went there, got pics and prices, put together a proposal for our company, and got us moved! Fuck yea, Walken. Our new building was a secured apartment building. Four floors, two pools, a parking lot, nice furniture. A working elevator and most importantly right across the street from Al Rashid Mall. Al Rashid Mall was a massive mall in our province, about the size of four Chicago O'Hare airports. It also had a Carrefour grocery store. We could now walk and get croissants, good Irish cheese, pasta sauce, etc. Before this move, we would have to take a taxi or walk about fifteen minutes to Tammi's. Fifteen minutes isn't bad,

I know, but in 120F weather carrying bags of groceries, it sucks balls. The day we moved from 18th Street to Al Khobar, we all packed up and moved at the same time in one big moving truck.

When offloading the truck and getting into our rooms we all were running up and down the stairs to see who got which kind of room. Small differences in layouts. Potter grabbed my arm and brought me down to his floor. He said, "You see that young Saudi kid in Walken's doorway, I used to fuck him, he's crazy." Already on our first day at this building Walken is bringing over tail. He was also smoking tree in his room with the door open. Lol. We had nice accommodation now and good grocery shopping so Walken could fuck whomever and as much as he liked and I could care less.

Walken, while ravaging the male youth of KSA, also helped us all out astronomically. He taught me how to home brew.

Let's make wine

Walken called me over to his room and gave me a shopping list. This is what you needed to brew. Was pretty easy. A case of grape juice, sugar, baking yeast. All available at Carrefour. At the cigarette shop across the street, we'd buy big water deposit bottles. Filled them half up with juice, heated the sugar and yeast and a bit of water in a pan on the stove, then funnelled it into the bottle, added the remaining amount of juice. Capped and turned it over several times for it to mix. De-capped it, threw a condom on top and poked some holes in the condom. In place of an airlock, a hole-punched condom worked fine. Two weeks later, you would have some very drinkable wine.

So I started my brewing. I would have about four large deposit bottles going at once. These would make about eight one-litre bottles per cook. A one-litre bottle would get about 120 riyals or $20-25. This helped finance my Bahrain trips for pork and real booze but it also provided nightly drinking, which was heaven sent.

Walken would add grapes, weird ocean spray juices, tea bags and various other unnecessary items to his cooks, all of which made his wine taste awful. I can confidently say mine was the best being made in our city. At least, from the various ones I had the pleasure or unpleasure of trying.

The bellhop's XMAS party

The bellhop had invited a portion of the teaching staff to an Xmas party at a friend's compound. I did not attend. One of the people he invited was a new teacher named Barry. Barry had recently arrived from Cambodia. Barry was a short lil troll-like gentleman with a what-highschool-am-I-going-to-shoot-up-next sorta look about him. Barry did not fit in well. He was way too familiar with people on arrival and didn't just watch, look, and listen to take in social cues of how to operate in KSA. He had left Cambodia under dire circumstances, which were never fully revealed. As the leprechaun at the air force would say, "Anyone coming from Cambodia …" He would then wave his finger from right to left several times while looking up and away at the corner of his eyes signifying that person is a no-no.

Cambodia is the most lawless country in Southeast Asia. Drugs are widely available during daylight hours in highly public places. Cambodia has also suffered from a sex tourism industry that has unfortunately been largely grossed at children by paedophiles. With the previous two aforementioned qualities combined it attracts the scum of the earth largely, white saviour-complex housewives, hippies, sex tourists, hopeless alcoholics with a splash of bar-stool prophets and lost souls.

Barry's first week at the air force he asked us all where to score drugs. I avoided him like the Hinderberg. At the bellhop's Xmas party Barry got super drunk, proclaimed himself Christ then told every women who wouldn't cough up their phone numbers that they were hopeless evil bitches. He then put on headphones and slithered into the compound pool fully clothed, while it rained.

Vomiting homemade wine at the Saudi air force base

Potter was a sauced-up guy (a semi-functioning alcoholic) and we would drink quite often. At this point and time, my crew mainly consisted of the Small Scotsman, Potter and the Bellhop. After work, Potter and I would do the exercise programme insanity, have dinner in our respective apartments then meet up again later for boozing, that is if Potter had not secured booty delivery for the evening.

One night we went pretty hard on the booze. If work was extra shitty, we would start drinking as soon as we were home at about 3 pm. We found out we could get access to the roof, which had a great view of the city. You could even see the causeway to Bahrain, which felt nice to look at.

The morning after we had wine'd up hard we were both still drunk. Potter was late for the van and I ran up to wake him. He was still faded, much more than me, from the previous night of bingeing. We got to work and tried not to stumble or speak as we reeked of booze. Thank God I did not have to teach there, I laid down in a break room all morning.

Poor potter had to go and deal with the animals. After his first period, he came into the break room. "My students totally know I'm drunk. I told them they could do whatever they want all day so they're being cool." I was still spinning and feeling awful. The teachers headed back to class and I stood up to go to the bathroom outside and immediately ran to the sink in the break room (I don't know why there were sinks in those break rooms but there they were) and projectile vomited all over the sinks. Bright purple Russian-spaceship-take-off vomit. The Saudi air force officers came in these rooms often and if they had done right then I would have been pretty fucked. Luckily, I only vomited for about 20 minutes then cleaned it all up.

Vomiting homemade wine at the Saudi Naval base. Sounds like an Offspring album.

Saudi dementia

After you spend enough time in KSA you start to get what the expats called "Saudi dementia". This was a constant agitated state where you were extra hypersensitive and completely nerve wracked. Doctors in KSA actually would use this term. There was not much you could do. You were easily triggered about every little thing. Basically you turned into an asshole. Burnt out. If you'd done over a year there, you were susceptible. Jersey and I both had it, as did our friends. Jersey had been living in the middle of the desert while most of our crew were in Al Khobar, an actual city.

Some people escaped into books. Others to the gym. Others to homemade moonshine called Al-raq that tasted like gasoline.

Some would go to Bahrain and bang hookers. Jersey had developed a taste for the "friends-of-the-causeway" in Bahrain. He also had a taste for not paying them the following morning. He wasn't shy about sharing this information. We would all call bullshit on him and tell him how horrible it was to dip out on these poor girls who were selling their bodies to him. He was making $8k a month at his job and he had no dependents so it was not as if he couldn't afford it. He was just, well, a complete asshole when it came to hookers.

On one particular afternoon when we were giving him shit for dipping out on a girl, his response went like this, "You guys think I give a fuck about some hoes? I don't give a fuck! I left that bitch out in the middle of the road on Christmas, IN THE RAIN!"

Karma ain't gonna be nice to him.

The misadventures of Potter

Potter loved his sauce. He would find his Zen while drinking. His Zen was about as peaceful as the Gaza Strip. He was a bookworm who read constantly, loved movies and cinema and men. He was a bit of a whore when it came to the fellas. When I first met Potter all I knew about him was that Jersey said he was one of the cool guys there. He was very quiet and well spoken and always had his face buried in a book. I knew he was in Bahrain every weekend so I asked him how he afforded it. He said he stayed with his friend at his apartment when over there.

"Oh? How'd you meet you friend there? Online? Like Facebook or something?"

"Grindr," he said.

"What's that? Like Facebook or something?" I asked.

"It's like Tinder but for gays."

I did a double-take and looked up. Potter was gay? You'd never have guessed it but, yeah, Potter was samesies.

Potter's first sexual encounter was in a dark closet at a house party with his then girlfriend at the time. She was on her period and didn't tell him. She had him go down on her. He did (first time). Left the closet to horrifyingly find out his face, shirt and mouth are covered in menstrual love blood. He said, "After that I wanted nothing to do with females ever again." Can't blame him.

On one special night with Potter drinking far too much homebrewed wine, he had one of his usual fuck buddies come over to his apartment. This time Potter had been hitting the bottle since work. He was wasted. A young Jordanian man came over and Potter was so wasted he started making fun of the Jordanian's thobe. The Jordanian realized Potter was way too fucked up this night for him, so he made to leave. Potter, in his boxers, wasted, tried to stop the Jordanian from leaving because he's a sexual deviant. The Jordanian broke free from Potter's grip, ran outside into our open parking lot, which connects from a main road to Al Rashid Mall. Potter still only in his boxers, ran after him, outside into the parking lot. Our security officers (two Indians) see a westerner run out of his building after a guy in a thobe. They ran out and tackled the Jordanian because they thought he robbed Potter. Potter was too wasted to even explain anything or come up with an excuse. The Jordanian told the guards his friend was too drunk to go to dinner so he tried to leave. Potter found this all out the next morning. How? The Indians brought him into the security office and showed him the video. LMFAO.

Saudi wraps

Jersey, who lived north of us, had a different work schedule so he went to Bahrain at different times. He worked for a large OSHA-type operation with about 100 foreign expats. Most of them older. They schooled him on different KSA hustles, similar to how Walken and the Bellhop had helped us out at the air force.

One hustle being how to smuggle pork and bacon back into KSA. One afternoon Jersey sent me a message telling me to check out his most recent Facebook post. The video was titled "My new cooking music". It was him cooking bacon on his trailer-park stove while in the background of the video the call to prayer was being announced in his city. I immediately shook my head at this.

What an idiot. One of the last things you want to POST on social media, which is heavily monitored in KSA, is you cooking bacon, especially during the call to prayer. It's such a slap in the face to Muslims. I immediately called him to tell him to take down the video and he told me, "You're the fifth person to tell me that." Not his brightest move. I immediately followed up with, "How the fuck did you get bacon!?!?"

One of the shops in Bahrain did "Saudi wraps". You'd go into the pork section, pick your products and ask for Saudi wraps. The deli guys would wrap up your bacon, ham, etc. in non-translucent deli paper, and then wrap it in saran wrap, then print fake price tags and labels on them for lamb chops, turkey, scallops, etc.

This was a game changer for us. We bought pounds and pounds of ham and bacon. At the customs checkpoint going over the causeway the agents would rarely go through the cars. If they did, they would see grocery bags filled with food. We would load up on food so the mislabelled pork packages would blend in better. It would just look like the kafirs had gone grocery shopping in Bahrain, which is a common occurrence.

Occasionally customs officials would look in our grocery bags and more or less search for hidden alcohol. Times were pretty good at this point. I had a nice one-bedroom apartment, as much wine as I wanted every night, compounds to go drink at and be social, extra cash for Bahrain runs from the lil homebrew operation and now regular pork and prosciutto.

On one trip back, Jersey and I loaded up hard on pork. We probably had five different wrapped-up types of bacon each. It was mixed in with our grocery shopping. We had done this about twenty times or more by now. We never brought booze back because that's just too risky and we had homebrew on lock. On this afternoon, we got to KSA customs on the causeway. Followed our normal procedure. Got out, opened up all the car doors, stood and waited. The agents usually came over and tilted their heads slightly and looked inside, stamped our pass and waved us on. It didn't happen that day. An agent came over and immediately told us to stand far away against a wall. We both looked at each other like fuck. He went through the trunk first, asking about Jersey's longboard and what it was for. Jersey explained it was like a skateboard. Jersey and I both tried to continue a conversation about longboarding in an attempt to keep our hearts from beating faster and reduce nervousness as the agent was now rifling through our groceries. We were behind the trunk at this point and we heard "WHAT IS THIS?!?!"

Well, that was a good year and a half in KSA, I thought, now I'm going to jail. As soon as we heard the word "what" come out the agent's mouth we both looked at each other with eyes like Alex from "A Clockwork Orange" opened like we were fucked. We walked over to the agent and he was holding up a bottle of Japanese green tea. Irish luck, thank you in spades. I told him it was just tea and pointed to the English at the bottom on the opposite side of the bottle. I invited him to open it and smell it, pointing out again that is says green tea printed on the bottle and it is indeed sealed and unopened. The agent laughed and said, "No problem, you're good, ok."

That was the last pork smuggling I did, for about eight months anyway.

Flyentology

I need about six drinks to get on a plane. Actually six drinks and three Xanax. Here is why.

When I was a pre-teen, my dad brought me into work. He was a captain for a commercial airline in the States and at that stage in his career he trained their pilots. This was pre 9/11; you could still go through security at airports if you weren't flying. And, if you were a captain, you could bring your kids into work. So he was doing check rides in airplane simulators. They are replicated cockpits of planes, button for button, inch for inch, that go up about four stories on hydraulics. They simulate every city on the windshield, which is a digital layout, they simulate every type of weather and every manoeuver a plane might encounter. They also simulate crashes.

As I was leaning over my dad looking at our city of Pittsburgh, he said, "Do you remember flight 427?"

"Yes of course."

Flight 427 was a flight that crashed near the Pittsburgh airport that killed everyone on board. Several classmates of mine had parents on the flight. It was a terrible ordeal to say the least. Yeah, of course I remembered. "This is what happened." My dad pressed a button and the simulator flipped over and with full-on sound effects and speed proceeded to simulate the crash. Now, I grew up flying free on standby because of my dad's job. Never in a million years did I imagine planes could or would ever do anything like what that simulator did that day. My legs were shaking for hours. Ever since then I have needed booze and Xanax to fly. It sucks.

We had a week off from the air force and I was flying to BKK to see my girlfriend. We had been trying the long distance thing and it was rough. I was supposed to be meeting her family the following morning in Bangkok. I was flying out of Bahrain and lay-overing in Abu Dhabi. At the Bahrain airport lounge, I was knocking back the vodka sodas for my first flight. Had about five or so and hopped on the flight.

The Small Scotsman had a layover at the same time as mine in Abu Dhabi so we planned on meeting in an Irish bar there. Success. I found the bar, which was a four-minute walk from my gate. The Small Scotsman arrives and we threw them back and back and back. I did about seven shots with him and was still a-o-k. I ran to my gate and made it in time. They were about to start boarding. I popped a muscle relaxer I had from a back injury that happened about a week prior. An announcement was made - the flight was delayed. I dozed off, woke two hours later and I could barely stand. I tried to get up and fell back down. The gate agents came over, helped me up and put me in a wheelchair. Security then came over and took me to the airport's doctor. They took my blood and gave me a drug test. I assured them I was not on any drugs. The test came back negative.

They took me out into the hallway and a tall American representative from Etihad Airways came over and asked what was up. I told him I'm scared of flying and I had had some drinks. He said, well, ok, I understand, but you've now missed your flight. "We're gonna get you a room so you can sober up." They took me to some sleeping capsules and I slept. I woke up without a plane ticket. I went to the service desk and explained what had happened and they refused to put me on another plane. They said I must book another ticket. I would have made this fucking flight easily had it not been delayed. I timed my drinking perfectly so I would have hit zombie mode once airborne. FUCK. I had not told my GF I was late. I found a Wi-Fi signal and made up a story about missing the flight. She woulda been SOOOOO pissed if she found out I missed the flight 'cos I was drunk. I think I told her years later what happened, accidentally. This was not the first time I had been denied boarding and missed flights. Those other stories are gonna have to be for another book.

Potter smokes crack

The Small Scotsman and I wake up in Bahrain one morning at our baller-ass Al Jabriya Suites hotel. Al Jabriya was one of the shittiest, cheapest hotels you could get in Manama. It did have bathtubs and kitchens though so that helped take away from its ghetto-ness. Al Jabriya cost about 280 riyals a night back then for a two-bedroom, which was about $70. It was also within walking distance of two of the most important places: Al Jazeera market (pork) and Bennigan's (bar open from 6 am to 3 am). We could get our pork fix from the grocer and hit Bennigan's for a normal drinking environment that wasn't filled with Chinese hookers bothering you the entire night. At Bennigan's two Guinnesses and a water would come to $60. The prices were not friendly but hey, these were the cards dealt in the Middle East.

Potter had stayed at a different hotel as he was trolling Grindr for samesies. The Scotsman and I cracked a beer and started tracking down Potter to come drink with us before we went back to KSA. I messaged Potter on Facebook and asked how his night went. "Smoked crack last night" was the only response I got. I immediately laughed aloud and asked for more info. He said it had to be told in person.

Potter arrived about thirty minutes later. Still drunk from the previous evening. He matched with a Palestinian on Grindr and went to his apartment. The windows were all covered in blankets.

Upon entering the room they had beers and his new friend asked, "Wanna smoke crack?" Potter said why not and then they, well, smoked crack.

Potter left the Palestinian after several more beers and proceeded to his next Grindr conquest. This particular Grindr conquest post crack-sesh was apparently some fancy Qatari who had some family that was a Baron or royal Sheik thing. When leaving in the morning the Qatari tried to give potter 100 BD (Bahraini dinar). That's about $260. Potter refused because he's an idiot. He would not shut up about how he was offered $260 as a thank-you-for-fucking-me payment.

"I can't believe I was offered money, these guys are mental. I WAS good though. He came a bunch. I'm a pretty good lay."

"Oh, you made a man cum?" I say. "Bravo Radcliffe, congratulations on making a male ejaculate, skills for days, Potter. Do you know how easy it is to make a man cum?"

The Scotsman interjects, "It's true, Potter, bragging about makin a man come ain't really giving ya many points. Try making a woman cum and we'll give you some credit, buddy."

Potter laughed and noded, as he knows it is true. Who the fuck goes around bragging about making men come? You throw a warm pancake at the right angle at a guy's face and he'll cum. Good for Potter though. Got laid and almost paid. We then go in on him for not taking the money 'cos it would have bought us all another night in Bahrain and got us another case of beer.

Walken takes pipe to Bahrain

Walken was a bit of a space cadet and scatter brained. He would regularly smoke hash in his apartment. I imagine he would lure his young boys into depraved sexual acts with his collection of chemicals. Do not forget: "Everybody plaaaaayz." On one of his boy trips to Bahrain he had piled in a car with his boys from Ha'al. Upon approach to Bahrain customs check he realized he had his pipe in the car. No, not a tobacco pipe. That devil's lettuce type of pipe. The dogs came out and started barking at their car and the officials made them all get out, with one dog going nuts. The Saudis were taken aside and frisked. They went up to Walken, asked for his passport, saw he is American and told him to get back in the car. Off they drove. Walken 1, Bahrain customs 0.

Pill party in Al Khobar

At the top of our building, on my floor, was a South African whom Walken new from times ago. I came back from a compound party with Bellboy one night and was still wanting to party. I had some wine and some Xanax and rang up Walken. "Yo, I have some wine but only a bit, you got any?" Of course he did. "I'm on your floor, come across the hall," he said. Walked out my apartment and knocked on my neighbour's door. We bust out our wine and started drinking. The S.A. had a massive outdoor porch as he lived in the penthouse. Big enough to fit forty people comfortably. The wine was running low and I asked if they wanted to do some lines of Xanax. Their faces lit up. I only had one left so we crushed it up and took down some mini lines. We were all feeling pretty good at this point and the S.A. returned from his room with three mini parachutes – some white powder crushed up finely in tissues and folded up like parachutes.

I asked what it was and they both insisted it was fine and to just take it. I had enough booze in me that I just wanted to keep the buzz going so I took it down and they followed suit. About twenty minutes later I was out on his porch listening to the Magic Tramps. Yeaaaaaaaaaa. They ended up carrying me home and I have never ever slept so well in my entire life. I dreamt about doing my taxes and all the math made sense. What was this wonder drug?

Seroquel. Seroquel is an anti-psychotic. It helped me sleep several nights in KSA. DO NOT EVER TAKE SEROQUEL UNLESS PRESCRIBED BY A DOCTOR. This will be further explained later.

Big T

Big T was a working girl in Bahrain. She was always at the bars and clubs. She also had the magic touch of being able to get you any booze delivered to your hotel at any time of the day or night. The Thais in Bahrain could find you booze when the bottle shops were closed. Our days off being Friday and Saturday we could only really buy booze Thursday afternoon after work. Friday is the holy day so no booze shops were open. Saturdays we would always be heading back to KSA so Thursday afternoon was it. If we didn't get booze by Thursday night then we were at the mercy of $12 Budweisers at one of the local bars unless we rang up a Thai for a booze delivery. Big T had hooked us up on more than one occasion. A lot of the guys in my crew all did time in Thailand so we could all speak Thai. After hearing some of the horror stories about what the Saudis and Bahrainis would do to the Thai girls at the clubs we always made an effort to try and buy them drinks if we ran into them.

Big T had now been gone for several months. We would usually see her at clubs or foreign restaurants around town. We heard she got kicked out of the country. I imagined for prostitution but wasn't sure. Then, out of the blue, we saw her one night at the Grand Prix in Manama. She came up and said hi to all of us. We asked what had happened. She said she had been at a club and a Bahraini had picked her up and taken her back to a hotel. At this point she was working him and he was a john or so she had thought. The guy fucked her and then took her downstairs where the police were waiting. She was arrested and deported.

Once back in Thailand she changed her name. Got a new passport. Came back to Bahrain and hit the bars again. Big T was unstoppable. Her nickname came from her teeth falling out over time. The "T" stood for toothless. We think she was smoking a lot of meth however that was never confirmed. The "big" part of her name came from how unusually tall she was. There you have it: "Big-T". Big T is now out the game and back in Thailand trying waitressing out. I hope she is doing well.

Maybe we become gorillas

The next batch of cadets that came through the air force was especially terrible. Extra kind of stupid you don't find often. I'm still astonished to this day that they managed to find their way out of their mothers' vaginas. Our reporting and meetings with the commander at this point were regular and depressing. He would tell us if we couldn't get the cadets to pass these classes they would shut down the programme. We had to get them to pass. The teachers and we did everything we could but these guys didn't even know the Arabic alphabet. How on earth were they supposed to learn a military course in English? I was walking by one of the old cadets from the previous year who was quite a standout student and he asked me, "Hey, how are the new cadets?"

"Not good, Metib, not good at all. They are still on Book 6 and they can't read." This was company 86 at this time.

Metib looked at me with a smile and said, " Maybe by company 90 we will have become gorillas." We both laugh.

In the late '90s King Khalid Air Base tried to introduce Saudization. This is where they restrict the work force to only Saudis. They fired all the foreign workers on the base, in total close to 500. In the four months they had only Saudis "working" there not one plane was able to take off. They had to rehire all of the foreign workers.

A sewage plant in Ras Tanura had 40+ Saudi employees on its books with not one Saudi working onsite. The manager, an Egyptian man, told us, "It is just better if they stay home, they're absolutely useless." The country was absolutely hopeless. The long-term expats there all said the same thing. They said that the Saudis would all go back to the desert. Once the oil money was gone and they couldn't afford to pay expats for their work at inflated salary rates, the expats would leave and the infrastructure of the country would fall with no local nationals to do even 15% of the jobs. They really were so lazy and useless that they didn't even need their thumbs.

At the time of writing this I saw a news article on TV: a Saudi women only realized when her plane was about to take off that she left her baby at her departure gate and the plane had to turn around and go back to the gate to get the forgotten baby.

The cadets couldn't even use a pencil sharpener. They would break them all because they would try to "clean" the eraser end of the pencil by putting it in the sharpeners.

Birthday take care:

On one of my birthdays we all went to Bahrain and got particularly extra fucked up. We went to the Elite 5 duplex. We tried to find some new clubs to go to and we did. Shot after shot, drink after drink and we all got separated. Finally I made it outside the club. Potter was there. "Potter, where the fuck are we? I'm way too fucked to be here." Potter said he didn't know but he was trying to bang a guy inside. I told him I was too fucked up to stay and was leaving. I would catch him back at the hotel. I was walking / stumbling out to the road and I couldn't recognize anything. None of the buildings. Nothing. I just saw these bright neon lights that looked like Vegas. What the fuck club did we go to? I just remember they played "Bulls on Parade" and told me I was dancing too violently. Pussies.

I finally, after about what might have been twenty minutes of stumbling and trying to ask for rides, saw an intersection I was semi-familiar with. My hotel was quite a walk away and I knew I was not in any shape to walk that far. There was a bar nearby where hopefully I could find some people I knew from

Manama or KSA. I made it there but could barely stand at this point. Finally, an angel grabbed my arm. It was M.J. M.J. was a girl I had met several months back. She used to work at Elite 5 and knew me from our various stays at her hotel. She would always give us free late checkouts and she could sometimes get us booze when we were out. Even if we were not staying at her hotel, she would hook us up with booze delivery. Her nickname came from the fact that she looked like a Filipino version of Michael Jackson. She had some very botched plastic surgery to her face. We had gone out on a few dates and she had told me I was the only man ever to have given her flowers. She had a soft spot for me but I wasn't all too into her to develop anything more than a couple nights of drinking and movies throughout the year.

She saw the state I was in and asked, "What the fuck is wrong with you? You're super drunk!"

"It's my birthday. I need to get home, please help me get home. I'm at Elite 5," I replied. She bought me three waters and made me down them. I was feeling better. She walked me outside and got a cab for us and took me back to the hotel and got me in my room. Thank God for M.J. We fell asleep. I woke up sometime later and had to piss. I opened the door and there was Potter fully naked ass-blasting some Bahraini, also fully naked. I immediately slapped both hands over my face and ran to the bathroom, screaming, "Fuck, guys ... sorry, but fuckin ay. There are two more bedrooms upstairs, you can't fucking go fuck in a closed room?"

That morning, being the day after my birthday, M.J. decided that her pink walnut would be a nice belated morning-birthday gift. While I wasn't particularly attracted to her, she was very sweet and when in the desert any water will do. Happy Birthday to me.

Potter and multiple hotels

Potter was a hotel connoisseur or at least he would like to believe he was. Occasionally he did book himself some nice hotels in Bahrain. He was always posting about terry-cloth bathrobes and the expensive linens his room would be adorned with. However, many of these hotels would not allow same sex visitors, they knew the score and no samesies would be taking place at their upscale establishments. On more than one occasion Potter would message us and ask if there were more rooms available at Al Jabriya.

"Why?" we asked.

"They won't let me bring him up! These fucking cunts."

This happened at least five times. Poor Potter and his two-hotels-a-night mishaps.

Potter moons the ladies

Potter and Jersey were staying at a high-end resort in Bahrain.

The high-end resorts all had bars and pools. Our usual haunts didn't have pools and certainly didn't have bars. If you wanted that then you'd be shelling out at least $150 a night for a studio single bed. Jersey and Potter were in the pool all day and Potter had hit his alcohol barrier where Griffendor becomes Slitherin.

He swam up to Jersey and said, "See those fuckin burka-wearin cunts? Watch this." Potter swam to the ladder opposite where all the females were swimming and gathering in the pool. He pulled his swimming costume down so his ass hung out, then proceeded to purposely fail at pulling himself out the pool. The women all got a nice two and a half minute show of Potter's bare pale white English ass. Low hanging fruit. The hate for Saudis was real.

The king's trip

Saudi Arabia has stupid money. Also, Saudis are not smart with their money. Jersey was over drinking one night at the new digs, well new digs to him. He told me he finally got his Saudi credit card. Your limit on Saudi credit cards was, like, 40% of your yearly salary. There was also no tax or interest in KSA since its haram. Islam with the win. We had always heard stories of the nurses in KSA (Filipina and South African) coming to Saudi, getting credit cards and going back home after three months and buying a car with the card and never returning. What was Saudi gonna do? Jack fuckin' shit.

So there's Jersey, three years in with his savings and a brand new credit card with a $40k limit. He said, "I want to go to Bahrain, buy gold and dip out. But I'm scared to fly with that much on me. I think I might just buy it in chunks and mail it."

"Dude that's a horrible idea. You wanna mail $40,000 worth of gold? You'll never see it again. Buy it and fly to Bangkok with someone who will hold half and then sell it on arrival," I say. I tell him about two guys I talked to at a restaurant in Phuket once. A father and a son. They got as many credit cards as they could in USA, flew to Thailand and bought gold, then sold all the gold for cash and lived off the cash. That's one way to do it. Jersey's eyes lit up. That's perfect but who will fly it with me.

"Um, I will mother fucker, are you kidding. Lez do it!"

For about a month, we planned it out. Jersey even got a second credit card for $20k. He went over to Bahrain and started to price out gold bullion. He tested the card to make sure it worked. I went up to Rasta Nora and got 2,000 riyals in cash from him so I could book my own ticket. I booked a one-way ticket from Bahrain on a Thursday night to arrive in Bangkok on the Friday morning and a return flight for the Saturday morning arriving back in Bahrain on the Saturday night.

We agreed for him to take me shopping at duty free and take care of partying in Bangkok and we'd call it even.

Thursday came and Waseem picked me up, took me over the border, and dropped me off at Bennigan's where I was to wait for Jersey. Jersey was on his final exit soon but was leaving early. His card was linked to his work. He was also leaving some unpaid dues at his trailer park. I still can't believe he lived at a trailer park in KSA. If he didn't arrive by 4pm I was to assume something had gone wrong at the border and abort the mission.

3:55 and Jersey finally arrived. "Dude, I got so much gold in my pockets right now," he said. He drove straight from work. We checked into Al Commodore Suites (Al Jabriya's little step-brother) and he showered and changed clothes. We packed up the gold and headed to the airport in his car. We arrived at the airport and I asked, "What about your car?"

He shrugged and said, "Saudi plates." His car was a rental from a company in KSA. When driving rentals with Saudi plates you kinda have a license to drive like an asshole or a Saudi, which is really the same thing. Whenever Jersey would pull a U-turn, cut someone off or do a spin-out he would shout, "Saudi plates, bitches." I laughed and asked him if he was sure he wanted to abandon his rental car there and he assured me he did.

Many people left KSA on bad terms purposely so they would never return. It was sort of like I hate it here so much I need to make sure I never return and do this to myself again.

We checked in, got our boarding passes, threw the gold in our bags, and made it through security and immigration without a problem. The custom agents asked me how I was and I respond "mia-mia", which is a Saudi term for 100-100 or very good. He said, "Oh, you are from KSA! Only Saudis say that. Have a good trip, habibi." We make it through. Golden, literally.

Next stop duty-free. IPhone 6s 30 gigs? Check. Beats By Dre? Check. I have been paid and I am happy. Hells, yes. We went to the Irish bar and waited for boarding. I was fairly faded by this point and we were both beyond stoked we'd made it this far. Only real hurdle left was customs in BKK.

We fell asleep on Gulf Air's 9 pm red-eye to Bangkok. Woke up upon landing. Went to the bathroom to move the gold into our pockets. Customs in Bangkok only scanned bags when not looking at their phones buried in some dumb game like Candy Crush. This was it, the final challenge. Neither of us had bags aside from small carry-ons. The only way they would stop us was if they wanted to do a random search, which I've never seen. We got through immigration, walked past the baggage carousel and headed towards customs. Deep breath. Bam. Walked straight through no probs. After exiting customs our faces lit up with smiles and the sort of celebrated high you get when you hit the lotto or get a movie contract or don't get caught smuggling pork into a highly draconian Islamic country. We literally started jumping up like we'd just done touchdowns.

Offloading gold in Southeast Asia works along international fencing. This fencing is fairly unregulated so it is set up to allow early-stage criminality with later-staged grey market trading. It's set up in such a way that it sanitizes portals for gold, minerals, art and antiques. Give with dirty hands and take money with clean ones. There is little documentation and almost zero enforcement. Jersey would have no problems offloading the gold in a variety of countries bordering Thailand.

With our successful entry into Bangkok we taxi to hotel and party all day. Halas.

Potter's adventures part two

When strapped for money there was a public bus you could take from 18th Street into Bahrain. It was a fucking pain though. It would take at least four hours each way. Everyone would have to get off the bus twice at passport control, each time this happened it would take an hour in each office. When trying to skin your wallet it was an option to save some riyal, as the bus was $10. If you did not have a crew to split a taxi over it would cost $120 each way. Potter was the bus master. On one such occasion when taking the bus back Potter had taken some ecstasy but was not feeling happy and lovely. He was pissed that he was on the bus, full of Saudis, save for one other British guy who worked on our base in a different programme. Once back on good old "chosen people" ground he went to Carrefour, for what I dunno. While at

Carrefour, he decided to vent his anger at the locals and proceeded to throw elbows at anyone in a thobe or burka. This didn't end well for Potter and he had to flee Carrefour but surprisingly he made it home. Saudis were far too lazy to run after someone.

DJ sponsorship: anytime

I had been doing really well getting shows while living in Saudi. I travelled so much during vacations I could hit up a promoter in any city between the Gulf of Arabia and the Pacific Ocean and get a gig. I had also started doing scratch videos on my IG account and got some attention from some DJ gear companies. They started sending me gear free as long as I used it in my videos. Saudi did allow me to save money, travel and keep doing music. All of which is a great combination.

Salacious Crumb gets the thrush

Do you know what the thrush is? I had never heard of it. It's a sex rash you get from ratchet pussy or ratchet dick. We had just come back from a long weekend and Salacious Crumb had gone back to see his indentured Thai wife, aka I-let-losers-cum-in-me. His wife had spent all the money he was sending back to her and his kid. $5,000 gone. That was a good amount of money for rural Thailand. Crumb was pissed and wouldn't shut the fuck up about it for weeks. Literally. "What time do you guys need to go to the grocer tomorrow?" asked Mohammed, our driver. "Well me wife is gonna keep spending me fucking money isn't she, so no point in going to the grocer is there, Mohammed." God I fucking hated this person. For weeks he endlessly moaned around with the world's most annoying pity-dick dangling out his mouth.

The first weekend back he went to Bahrain to the dirtiest, nastiest bar in all of the Middle East. The Dubliner. It was filled with Chinese hookers who had that thirty-types-of-semen-in-their-stomach look. He found a hooker he fell for and started banging her without a condom. He got thrush and wouldn't shut up about it. Went to a doctor in KSA and got a cream he and his lady were supposed to use to rid themselves of it. He forgot to bring it over to her for weeks but kept fucking her raw and re-contracting thrush. He couldn't keep his hands out his pants for weeks dealing with his itchy goblin cock.

Salacious plays immortal technique for Al Sami

Like the small child he was, whenever he was in a pouting mood, which was always, he would blast loud music in the break room. No headphones. He such a cunt. The smoker's break room consisted of The Mad Hatter, Mr Al Sami and Salacious. After week one of Salacious I had exited this break room and started smoking outside. Mr. Al Sami was in his 60s and from Somalia. He wore a long thobe with a head dress. He was a wonderful co-worker. He helped me learn the Arabic alphabet. Everyone liked him, he was a soft wise soul amongst a heard of crazies. He has now since passed, RIP. My locker was still inside the smoker's room though so one day I walked in and there was Crumb blasting Immortal Technique on his computer. "Aids infested child molesters ain't sicker than me" coming from his computer. The look on Al Sami's face. Fuckin crumb. The only time I've seen Al Sami bothered in two years was 'cos of fucking crumb.

Potter ODs at Damam airport: Ramadan

It was our second Ramadan. This time the Small Scotsman and I were gonna hit Vietnam, Thailand and Cambodia. I had been to Cambodia before and was happy to go again. Vietnam would be the new country for this Ramadan and my good friend Jake would be joining us.

Potter would be returning to the UK to see family then do a Euro trip for the summer. I was hunting the South African neighbour, as I wanted Seroquel for my flight. Three hours before the flight I ran into him in the hallway.

"I heard you're looking for me," he said.

"Yes, I am. Do you have any …" He stopped me and said to hold out my hand. He dropped four Seroquel in my hand and wished me a fond Ramadan.

I was packed and ready to go. Headed down to Potter's and he wanted a pill to sleep on the plane. I cannot remember if we were drinking or not. I split a Seroquel with him and we got the Small Scotsman and headed to the airport. About ten minutes from the airport I noticed Potter nodding off pretty hard in the taxi. We got there, bounced out and got in line, dealt with the box packers and were standing in line for our tickets. Potter looked really out of it but ok enough.

KA-THUD. Gasps and screams from behind me. I spun round to see Potter on the floor turning bright blue. FUCK. NO. FUCK. NO. The Scotsman and I immediately rushed down to him and tried to wake him up, yelling and slapping his face. Nothing. He was turning bluer and all I could think was I've just killed my friend and he's going die. About two minutes passed and he finally opened his eyes, the blue starts to fade. "What's going on?" we hear from the crowd watching us. Who the fuck is that? Oh no, its fucking Florida. "Hey guys what's going on? Is he ok?" Florida asked. We've got Potter up and standing and now airport staff and security were there assessing the situation. Potter said he was fine and took a step and passed out again, limp on the floor and turning blue again. Fuck me. Oh, Fuck me. "Should I call Aziz?"

Florida asked. Simultaneously the Scotsman and I screamed at Florida, "NO!"

Potter was still passed out and they brought a nurse over, finally. The nurse was in full burka with a face veil covering the entire front part of her face, this meant you couldn't even see her eyes, she was full-on Darth Vader. Hands fully covered too. She had water and was dampening his forehead. Finally he opened his eyes and gasped for breath. The first thing he saw was this black-cloaked figure holding him. Can only imagine how crazy that must have looked to regain consciousness and the first thing you see is a Starwars villain mumbling Arabic to you. Finally Potter is up, sitting and getting some colour back. I hightailed it to the bathroom and flushed the remainder of the Seroquel I had in my pocket. Shaking uncontrollably as I flushed the two pills I had left. I headed back out and called Walken. "Walken, what the fuck is Seroquel and has anyone had bad reactions to it? Potter just fucking OD'd at the airport." Walken was zero help. "Nooooo, everybody fine with it, maybe it was something he ate," he said. Thanks, Walken.

Potter was now standing and full colour had returned, well, all the blue had gone, he was just extra English pale at this point. I asked the gate agent at the check-in counter to move me next to him on the flight, which he was happy to do. Potter was stressing that they would not let him fly. He kept telling them, "I'm fine. I need to make this flight. I have connections to make in Qatar and I have to be on this flight, please." They didn't seem to have any problems with it so they let him check in and get his ticket. We made it through security and immigration. Scotsman and I weren't taking our eyes of him at this point. We got to Popeye's and made him eat. He looked ok at this point. We were downing him with Louisiana fried goodness and water. Made it onto the plane but they did not sit me next to him. I must have gotten up like four times to check on him during our forty-minute flight to Qatar. I had the air hostesses check in on him to. We all made it to Qatar ok and the Scotsman and I hit up the caviar bar for vodka and beer. I fucking needed a drink after the last four hours like never before. Potter was happy as a pig in shit. "Feel fine now, fellas, gonna go catch my flight. Wish me luck," he said.

"Potter, you gotta message me as soon as you land at Heathrow and let us know you're all right. Ok, promise us. DO NOT FORGET," I insist.

"Ok, relax, Mum. I'll message once in Heathrow."

Couple of beers later we boarded our flight and arrived in Bangkok. I still felt horrible when landing. Got a sim card and messaged Potter immediately. He'd already arrived and said he slept amazingly on his flight. Thank motherfucking God. That horrible feeling followed me for days and the majority of the Ramadan trip. What a way to start summer vacation. Little did I know it was about to get just as fucked up for another close friend within hours.

Master Shake gets rolled: Ramadan

The Scotsman and I rested for a couple of hours. I was still processing how fucked the last 24 hours had been. I had plans to meet Master Shake and his buddy at a beer garden around the way. The Scotsman and I hopped on the sky-train and headed to Phra Khanom station about two stops away. Shake was already there with his buddy throwin back expensive craft beer. We joined and told him about our crazy twenty-four hours. Not much was new with Shake. He was still at the same job and playing basketball every day and smoking copious amounts of ganja. It got to be about 9 pm-ish and Shake said he had to go pick up from his latest weed spot one stop away in Thong lor. He invited us to roll along and we both said no fucking way. The absolute last thing I wanted to be around was any sort of illegal activity, especially if it involved drugs.

The Scotsman wanted to go to a girly bar in Nana and I was dead tired so I went home, Scotsman went to Nana and Shake went to score.

The next morning I got a text from Shake. "Dude, I got arrested last night, need money."

Shake the captain of bad decision making. "Fuck, bro, what happened?" I responded.

The cops were waiting for him right outside his new pickup spot. He had been going to this reggae bar the past year and picking up his tree there. This particular night as soon as he walked out after buying, six police rolled up to him and his friend and cuffed them both and took them to the station. They had them sweat for about two hours. Telling them that they would receive twenty-year sentences for the weed. Finally Shake was like, "What the fuck, guys, how much?" They told him 500,000 baht, about $15,000. He laughed, there was no way he could get that money. They said he'd need to get a large amount. He told them only his wife could access any money. They called his wife and she came down to the station. Once she got there, they let his friend go. After hours of negotiation, they agreed on 80,000 baht. A little under $3,000. His wife had to call her family and get the money sent to her account, then go to the ATM and withdraw it for the cops. Most expats living in Southeast Asia do not have this type of money lying around. At least not the ones whose primary daily activities are basketball and spliffing.

As soon as the cops got the cash, they celebrated. They literally shut off all the lights, walked across the street to the beer garden and began drinking. All this in eyeshot of Shake and his wife. No shame at all.

It's a common story in Thailand. Dealers and police working together. So they set up these busts. Dealer gets his product back, a cut of the payoff, and the cops make half their yearly salary in a night. The average police salary in Thailand is 8,000 baht a month. That's under $300. They have to buy their uniform, gun and bike. If you see a cop in Thailand on a nice bike he got that from one place.

Helping Saudi girl with HW

My driver Waseem called me up one night randomly. Told me he had a customer that needed help doing a homework assignment for her college class. Asked me if I could help her. I said sure. She called me up but was too shy to speak so we switched to texting on WhatsApp. She needed help developing a marketing campaign for a grocery store. I came up with a diet drink for females and drew up a small promotional campaign she could use. Once I finished writing it up and sent it to her she immediately started an interview on me. She asked if I was single, if I wanted to get married and if I would be willing to marry her and convert to Islam. Strange days. From what I can remember I told her I was planning on moving out of KSA or something along those lines so I was unable to think of marriage at that time.

Don't stay during Ramadan

Do you remember how I said you should never stay in KSA during Ramadan? Those that did, with very, very, very few exceptions, literally went crazy. During daylight hours you might as well not even go outside because you could literally do nothing. Nothing was open and if you were seen even drinking water you'd get arrested, best-case scenario. Our regional gremlin, aka Barry ,decided to stay during Ramadan, eight weeks, in his room, by himself. We arrived back refreshed and rested and ready for another year. We were all astonished at how Barry stayed the entire time. Bad move, Barry. Barry started walking outside in the parking lot during the day talking to himself. He would use very large gestures like he was arguing with someone who was clearly not there. I went to Aziz and told him he needed to keep an eye on Barry 'cos he was clearly losing it. We had a meeting that week where Barry suggested that our entire staff start wearing Saudi Military Uniforms so the cadets would respect us more.

A weekend or two later Barry went to Bahrain and wasn't heard from for weeks. Aziz called me and another guy into his office. He said, "Read this email." Barry had written Aziz an email proclaiming himself as God and that Aziz's inferior Islamic God was a hack. The rest of the email prophesized himself as the next Jesus and so on and so forth. Aziz then asked what he should do with this. We said we had no idea. "We told you he was losing it, Aziz." Aziz didn't know what to do. One thing he could have done was call the Mutawa on him and gotten him in some heavy, heavy trouble, which he did not.

Two days later Aziz got a phone call. It was a hotel owner in

Bahrain. Barry was naked, running around the hotel and refusing to pay his tab and check out. Why not call the cops? Well the owner of the hotel wanted to get paid, that's why. Aziz sent one of our drivers, older Mohammed, over to Bahrain to see what was going on and perhaps remedy the situation.

Barry was indeed shit-faced but manageable. Mohammed got his credit card and paid the hotel and wrangled Barry back to KSA. Barry refused to come back to work so Aziz rightfully fired him but he wouldn't leave. He refused to leave the country. We tried to talk sense into him and all the while he was proclaiming himself as Jesus. After a few days we convinced him to leave because he was going to be arrested if he didn't. A year later we saw him back in Dammam sitting on some steps outside Carrefour. Saudi attracts a special type of crazy. One of the best descriptions I heard about what happens to you when you live in KSA was this: Whatever is wrong with you when you come here, Saudi will only amplify it and make it worse. Truth all day.

Converts fighting

A common trait among the American converts in KSA was fighting with one another over who was more Muslim. This next story is not that. We had two converts at the air force at this time. One of whom I got along with great. He was from the same city in America that I was from and he was a solid mellow dude. He was also the only person I've seen in my entire life who was bigger than Jersey. This guy looked like he ate weights. If Schwarzenegger and the mountain from "Game Of Thrones" fucked and had a baby, he would be this baby. He was built like fucking Everest. He had been in the Middle East for the past twenty-five years. Spoke, read and wrote fluent Arabic. Had lived in Yemen, Egypt, Kuwait, everywhere. Had four wives. Prayed five times a day. He was the real deal. He also never cared when we talked shit about the Saudis or asked questions about Islam. We'll call him Pittsburgh. Potter used to say Pittsburgh talked like a 70s porn star. Potter and Walken both crushed hard on Pittsburgh. It was funny to see Potter get all triggered when I'd make fun of him in front of Pittsburgh in the break room.

Pittsburgh was constantly being tailed by Becky, the lil troll convert that nobody liked. He was such a soyboy vegan snowflake cuck with people. Zero social skills. Becky didn't bother me as much as he bothered others, other than the fact he hated Florida unjustly and he made fun of people with Down's syndrome once. That's fucked. I grew up and was friends with several kids who had Down's syndrome. If you're twenty-nine years old, working as teacher and are a self-proclaimed Muslim you're a piece of shit if you feel the need to make fun of people with Down's syndrome. If you're not any of those things and still make fun of people with mental disabilities you're also a piece of shit, just like Becky.

Becky would follow Pittsburgh around and constantly ask questions about Islam. Pittsburgh would try to tell him that he would never learn Islam on Google. He needed to learn Arabic and start studying more.

While we were all on our Hajj vacation in September, Pittsburgh's mother died. He stayed in the States to attend the funeral and take care of family business. He returned to work about a week after we all got back. The air force fired him. This was very strange as he was a fluent Arabic speaker and a solid Muslim. Pittsburgh was black and even though they're brown people, the Saudis are as racist as it gets. If it had been a white co-worker they wouldn't have said shit. If you aren't a male-Saudi-Sunni then you are utterly worthless to them. Women are below housecat in that country. Because Pittsburgh came back late this was their excuse to fire him. This was the only teacher they had that spoke Arabic and could get the bottom barrel of cadets to understand their material so they would one day not Allahu Akbar themselves in our grocery store.

Pittsburgh called immigration after I told him to research the labour laws in Saudi. "You can speak Arabic, they won't give you the run around there, call 'em up and find out if it's true." We had always heard you couldn't be fired in KSA. You would always get sixty days notice and you just had to be on site and not work post-firing. Well, this was indeed true.

Pittsburgh called immigration and they confirmed it. He told our company's supervisor if you want me outta here you will pay me two months' salary and a plane ticket. Our supervisor wasn't used to such directness or education. He was shaken. There was nothing they could do so Pittsburgh came into work every day and sat in the break room getting paid. And rightfully so. How the fuck you gonna fire someone after their mother dies???

One day our air force supervisor asked Pittsburgh, even though he was standing down, if he could help out during the test the following day. Pittsburgh smiled and said, "Sure, whatever you need."

The teachers the following day were testing and I was in the break room with Cornell and Slum Dog. Pittsburgh walked in and said, "I'm done, man. I am done with these crazy people!" "What happened?" we asked. Pittsburgh just started to shake his head.

Potter then came in and burst out laughing at Pittsburgh. "Did you tell em?" he asked.

"Naaaaah, I ain't tell em yet."

"Guys, what the fuck, tell us what happened."

Potter proceeded to tell the story: "I'm in my room checking test papers and I hear Becky screaming 'help, help, help' then I see him run down the hallway to the commander's office."

Jesus fucking wept. Can this kid be anymore bitch?

Later that day I heard both versions from both Pittsburgh and Becky.

Knowing them both and hearing both sides, here are the events of what happened.

Becky was lead proctor and Pittsburgh was helping him out as his number two. At the end of the test Pittsburgh went up to Becky and said, "You good? Cus I'ma bounce now." There were usually two teachers per room for testing. One to watch for cheaters and one to be lead proctor and handle distribution of materials, check the tests, their order and name accuracy. Becky was lead proctor so by all accounts he should have let and encouraged Pittsburgh to bounce post-test. He did not. When Pittsburgh asked to leave Becky said to him, "You know you try to be this big bad Muslim but you're really not."

Pittsburgh replied, "The fuck you know about Islam, you're just here 'cos you're trying to not be gay."

Becky then stood up with all his 140 pounds of peacock feathers and tried to chest up to Pittsburgh who laughingly pushes him into some desks.

Becky's account differed here. He said after Pittsburgh pushed him, he held the door shut and wouldn't let him leave. That's when Becky yelled for help … several times.

That is the only discrepancy. Everything else was agreed upon by both sides. Becky then ran to the commander's office. Informed the commander that he had just been attacked, then Becky fucking called the U.S. consulate and said his life was in danger. Dictionary, meet your definition of bitch. We were all on the floor laughing at this point in the break room when the commander came in. We quickly collected ourselves and the commander came to the table and put both hands down on the table like some Frank Underwood shit, said something to Pittsburgh in Arabic and they both burst out laughing.

BAE

Another defence company worked on the air force base and they too had their share of crazies. We were talking with their manager after we noticed one of their older employees hadn't been seen in weeks.

"Where'd that one guy go?" we asked.

"He was actually chased out of the country."

This older man had fallen in love with a young taxi driver. The taxi driver's father found out about it and went to their compound and tried to fight him. He wasn't let inside the compound. The father threatened to kill him and or go to the police (the latter not likely as his son was one of the two guys fucking in this never-meant-to-be love story). His company didn't want any more trouble or to get the rep that they had gay employees, so they helped him escape to the airport at 3 am. They drove out with him in the trunk of a car to avoid the angry father who was waiting outside the compound still huffing and puffing. They got him to the airport and put him on a one-way flight home.

Another winner that this defence company had was a younger fellow whose name I never even got, or cared to. He was brought into his regular yearly appraisal and review. His manager asked him the usual questions and gave the usual feedback. Right before the end his manager told him he heard he and his roommate were having plumbing issues and he'd be sure to get it fixed for them. The guy asked, "What plumbing issues?" His manager went on to explain his roommate had said that the shower drain didn't work properly and the water never completely went down the drain.

The employee said, "Oh, no need for a plumber, I know what the problem is."

"Tell us then, will you?" his manager (British as well) asked.

"Well I take me shits in the shower in the morning and stomp em down the drain, I reckon that's what's likely stuffin up the pipes, ay? Should probably stop that I should, get our pipes back in order."

Fired that day.

Dubai

A friend of mine was DJing in Dubai one weekend and I hadn't seen him in over ten years. Potter and I flew over for the weekend to see my buddy and party. We got to our hotel who then upgraded us out of nowhere to one of the presidential suites. Our balcony was the entire length of two sides of the hotel. It wrapped around and was big enough to play a legit game of roller hockey on. Massive. Four bedrooms, four bathrooms, a kitchen, massive living room and a maid's room. It was easily the biggest place I have ever stayed in out of 800+ hotels. There was only one other hotel room on our floor, taking up the other two sides of the hotel.

We went to meet my buddy at his hotel pre-club. Had a couple drinks then headed to the club. Potter and I got shots, danced and enjoyed thoroughly. I waited for my buddy to settle up after the club shut down. Potter had gone off to find some booty to shag. My buddy and I had a couple more drinks then called it a night.

Next morning I had plans to meet up with a girl I matched with on Tinder prior to arriving in Dubai. She had the biggest ass I ever done seen and wanted to party. She was from Cyprus and invited me over to her place for the afternoon to drink beer. Great, perfect. I brought a couple beers from my room, hopped a taxi and got there. Sent her a message when I was outside and she texted me to come on up.

I arrived at the door and a young African girl opened the door about an inch and asked who I was. I said I was there to meet Stephanie.

"Is Stephanie here?"

"Yes, she's in the back room, come in."

As soon as I stepped inside, the girl slammed the door and

threw her back against it and fifteen large Nigerians sprang up from behind a mid-level wall divider. I immediately looked back and the door was blocked. They all rushed me. The entrance to the apartment comprises a small hallway about five feet in length. Walls on both sides. The wall stops at five feet on your right and there was a mid-level wall about four feet high going another six feet dividing the entrance hall from the kitchen. The fifteen Nigerians came from behind this mid-level wall and the back bedrooms. There were five of them on my person with two holding the front door shut and the rest behind them all yelling. "Where is your money? Give us your money!!!" I tried to calm them down but that didn't work. I looked behind me again and I reckoned I could probably get the door open but not without getting some nasty cuts and bloodied up, and that was a best-case scenario. So I told them to hold on and I'd get some money. I then thought I could try to fake a heart attack and they'd maybe just kick me out? That didn't work. I grabbed my left arm and pretended to be having chest pains. They slapped me in the face several times and I reluctantly gave them my cash. I told them I needed to keep at least 100 riyals so I could get home and they did let me keep that.

I took the elevator downstairs and saw the receptionist. He was 35-40 years old, Nigerian as well. I told him what had happened and to call the police. He went upstairs to the room and came down again. He said that there were only two people in the room and if I want to call the police I would have to go back up and identify who stole the money. Yeah, right. Go back up and identify them???? That doesn't sound shady at all. Having suffered in KSA for this money, I wasn't about to let them get away with this so I begrudgingly went back up with the receptionist to identify them. In the elevator it occured to me how ridiculous this was, that I had to go back up. It then occurred to me that this receptionist being from the same country could be in on it. I pulled out a pen and looked him dead in the eye and said, "If you're in on this and you guys fuck with me again I'm taking your eye out first, I promise."

He got super offended and pleaded with me that he was certainly NOT a part of anything and he was only trying to help me. We got to the room, one man opened the door and said no one else was there. I told the receptionist they were all in the back room and to go inside to check. The receptionist said he needed to check the back room or he would have to call the police. The first man yelled at the rest of them and they all came out. I explained to him that those were indeed the people who took my cash.

The receptionist now called up a security guard. This security guard was about four foot tall and clearly not going to be able to do anything to these people in the apartment. The security guard was also clearly not paid nearly enough to put up with a gang from Lagos. The receptionist told them they had to give me my cash back or he would call the police. Several of them tried to make a run for it (to where, I don't know). My pen was in my hand, fist tight, ice pick gripped, ready to take out eyes if they ran through.

They were all visibly pissed I had returned and not fucked off. After going back and forth with them, and several failed attempts by them to run to the elevator, they finally threw the majority of my money at me on the floor. I picked it up and thanked the receptionist and security guard. Got a cab and went home. Wait till Potter heard this story. As soon as I was back I cracked open about two beers and chugged em on down immediately. I told Potter and his boy-toy what happened and we celebrated my meagre attempt to get my monies back. After thinking about it, they had a pretty good hustle. They had a fake Tinder account and would lure Emirati guys over to party. An Emirati who isn't legally allowed to be in a room with another women alone (who isn't family or his wife) would never ever call the police, because he himself would be in shit with the law. They must have raked in tons and tons of loot from poor unsuspecting Emirati guys. If you're ever in Dubai using Tinder, meet them at a mall or restaurant or club, do not go to their room!!!!

Palestine trip

In November we were gifted two weeks away from the air force.

Slumdog, Cornell and I went to Jordan, Palestine and Israel. It was a fantastic trip that we did mostly by land. We flew into Amman, Jordan, via Bahrain, took a bus to the boarder of the west bank, crossed into Israel and took a two-hour desert taxi to Jerusalem and then a train to Tel Aviv.

The border crossing from Jordan to The West Bank is one of the most notorious border crossings in the world, the Allenby Crossing. We didn't know what to expect but we knew it wouldn't be smooth or quick. To enter Saudi Arabia you cannot have any Israeli visas or Israeli stamps in your passport. This is true for several Muslim countries. I had two passports with me so I had a backup. Slumdog and Cornell did not. And Slumdog and Cornell were stopped. They are both mixed race and Cornell kinda has an angry-terrorist look about him, even though he is one of the sweetest guys I've ever met. He looked mad suspect if you didn't know him though. They were both taken aside and questioned at length. Israeli guards ran all the checkpoints going in and out of the west bank. They questioned us about our Saudi visas and asked what we did there, how long we worked there and what we planned on doing in Israel. The blacklist of Israel visas and stamps in Muslims countries had become such a problem for travellers that Israel only gave out visa cards. It had your picture on it and you had to carry it in your passport and give it back when exiting. So we dodged that bullet as far as possible denial of re-entry into KSA was concerned.

Once in Tel-Aviv we partied on the beach all night until sunrise. Tel Aviv is easily one of my favourite cities. The art, the vinyl, the people, all dank. We then took the train back to Jerusalem to do some sightseeing. Jerusalem has the world's best lemons. And a few really good record shops in closets inside clothing stores. The local shop owners would bring us fresh tea while Cornell and I dug through their record collections.

We got a taxi to take us into one of the backways to Bethlehem for the day, which is in modern-day Palestine. Palestine is very run down. The first thing we noticed when we crossed into it was the dilapidated housing and lack of structure and economy. They had a fake Starbucks in Bethlehem, the only building that had windows and lights. They jacked the exact Starbucks logo but spelled the name wrong. When driving around Bethlehem we got to see some of Banksy's artwork, which was dope. We also went to the apartheid wall which was littered with graffiti cans and artwork from some of the world's most prolific graffiti writers. If you get the chance to go, you should. The Palestinians could really use some tourist dollars amongst other things.

The next day we toured old town Jerusalem. Jerusalem is home to Christians, Jews and Muslims. Each with their own quarter. It's pretty segregated to say the least. We stopped to get a kebab on our way out of old town. The kebab shop was run by three Palestinians guys. The Palestinian guys could tell Slumdog was gay. He wore scarves and had a very clean fashion sense and spoke very effeminately. They joked with him a bit and asked where we were from. We told them we worked in KSA. The guy spit on the floor and said FUCK the Saudis. The other two nodded in agreement. He went on to say that the Saudis are the biggest joke of the Middle East. They think they are better than all the other Muslims because they have the kabala and the oil. "What have they done for Palestine with that money? NOTHING! What have they done for Palestinians with that money? NOTHING! We hate them." He was passionate about his hatred for them and we three could all relate. He then ended with a goodbye and wished us well and then he said, "My friend, I promise you one day the Saudis will get theirs and they will kneel down and kiss the ring of the Palestine."

Bringing Israeli records back into KSA

By this time I had successfully smuggled copious amounts of pork, Xanax, Valium and a plethora of other benzodiazepines into the kingdom. The pork was wrapped with covers stating lamb, turkey, etc. and the benzos were usually accompanied with an old script or two should they ask about them. Bringing Israeli records back in was another story. The covers all had Hebrew on them. In addition to these Israeli records I had a number of religious items for my mother and for her brother who is a priest. These had printed pictures of the Blessed Virgin Mary and Jesus. If customs went through my bags this time I really would be fucked without a hope in hell. Fortunately we flew back into Bahrain. I buried the records in between other vinyl I had purchased on the trip and wrapped the religious ish in my clothes and hoped for the best. We bought a bottle of wine at the Bahrain airport and pounded it. Cornell had Israeli records too so we wanted a lil extra liquid courage before going across the causeway. Waseem picked us up and we breezed right through.

Change of jobs

Shortly after the West Bank trip I got a call from a local contractor that was hiring. The salary was double and I was hungry as hell for this job. I got it and moved across the street and starting working for the Royal Saudi Navy under a different contracting company. They had a compound, company cars and health insurance. It was a real job with a real company.

Back to do the real deal physical visa

I went to Washington D.C. and had to go through all the real tests people go through for a legit KSA visa. Background tests, blood, urine, faecal tests. The lot. The best part was the thirty days in between jobs. Got to see the family. Drank beer. Ate pork. While in D.C. got to see my college friend who was now producing some of the finest music in hip-hop. This guy does Nas, Wu tang, the lot. We had been working lightly on an instrumental album the past year but now had time to put in. I stayed at his house and we crushed out an album in a week. It was great. Several years' worth of binded, strangled creativity nutted out in four nights. Love me Americans. I was recording samples on my phones daily. We went through seven pages of samples and picked out the best thirty for the album. It's called "Thugee", keep your eye out for it.

This new contract was for the Royal Saudi Navy. Their cadets were far fucking worse. 79% of them were court appointed into the navy. I thought no way possible that the cadets could be any worse than the air force. Wrong. As. Fuck. These lil fuckers threw literal shit, human shit at their teachers. Who the fuck throws shit at people? Saudis, that's who. They went to their bathroom, shit in their hand and threw it out a window at a group of teachers. Well played Saudi, well played.

The compound life

Minus the awful cadets, I had finally made it. I was on a compound. When I arrived at the Dammam airport with my fancy real-deal iqama full-on legal Saudi visa, all I knew was that I was going to be on a compound with up to four potential roommates. I had friends of friends at this compound and company but no one I knew personally. I arrived at the compound with a driver they had sent for me. He took me and my bags and opened the door to an unoccupied two-bedroom apartment. FUCK YES.

The next day I had orientation. There was one other new guy there, named Mario. Mario looked a little bit younger than me, so about 32-33. We sat through orientation, just the two of us and two managers at a coffee shop on the compound. Easy times.

Mario and I became good friends. He knew some guys who had been working at our spot so they would give him, and vicariously me, the inside scoop on ish at work and on the compound. Nobody was brewing there unfortunately. A quick run to the grocer and I would fix that.

Mario and Jesse

Mario introduced me to Jesse, a friend of his working at our company. Jesse was a tall, very effeminate awkward guy from Atlanta. Mario and Jesse were both samesies but not together. I found out that Mario was actually 45 years old, the fuckin guy looked like he was 27! Jesse was pretty jealous of Mario 'cos Mario would get lots of ass regularly and Jesse was a bit of a drama queen and at least from what I saw, didn't have any game.

We all went over to Bahrain together for a day of drinking. It was the first time all three of us had gone drinking together. If any of you readers of this book happen to be homophobes I highly suggest you quit that shit and get up on 2019 with the rest of the human population. Gay dudes, samesies, queens, etc. are some of the most entertaining and funny people I've ever partied with. You don't have to put a penis in your mouth when hanging out with samesies. Ever in a foreign city and trying to score drugs? Go to the biggest gay bar, you will find them. These guys party harder than anyone else or any other scene I've been privy to. So, Jesse, Mario and I started out the day at Bennigan's. Jesse went on to say how he hated being single and couldn't find any men to marry.

I told him I knew a tonne of gay single guys at the air force. I whipped out Facebook and showed him Slumdog and Cornell but he kinda "mehs" them. I then said I knew another guy who looked like Harry Potter who was single but not looking for a boyfriend. Jesse and Mario looked at each other and fell silent.

Mario asked, "Is he British?"

I said, "Yeah, why?" They both looked like their mouths were filled with hot air and they just started shaking their heads at one another. I was like, "What! What is it? You guys know Potter!?" Mario asked to see a picture. I showed him. His eyes closed and he bowed his head and almost simultaneously cried and laughed.

Jesse asked Mario, "Is it him?"

Mario said yes, cry-laughed once more and took a big swig of his beer. "It's definitely him," Mario confirmed again.

"From the night with the dead body?" asked Jesse.

"Yes, the same guy from the dead body night," Mario said.

The dead body

The samesies crowd partied hard in Bahrain. Primarily they used two mobile phone apps – Grindr and Scruff – to engage in consensual male-on-male fornication. One night Mario and Jesse linked up with some rich guy who lived in Bahrain and had a condo there. Don't remember what nationality they said he was but the guy would throw big orgies at his place. Gay dudes love orgies and they have them a lot. Like a fuck ton. So the story goes: Mario and Jesse were at this guy's condo doing their thing. Potter showed up. Everybody was fucking except for Jesse. Eventually the owner passed out and Potter and Mario kept fucking. They saw Jesse looking over and I guess half-ass asked him if he wanted to join, but Jesse picked up that he'd been pity invited. I'm sure there is some funny gay term for that, a pity invite for an orgy. Being asked to join in an orgy but the inviters really don't want you to join so you decline 'cos you know they just asking to be nice. There's gotta be a term for that.

So Jesse said no and Mario and Potter continued making the beast with two backs. When Potter left, probably to go fuck again somewhere else, Mario came out and saw Jesse has caught feelings. Mario being his friend felt ubber shitty 'cos he knew the pity invitation was just that. There was a mix of drugs circulating throughout the night and emotions were running up and down, hot and bothered.

Mario was getting sick and couldn't take it and was kinda about to have a panic attack so he said he had to leave. He took the elevator down and was walking across the reception hall to the condo entrance when a Saudi ran up to him, grabbed Mario's arm, had a heart attack and died. The Saudi collapsed on the floor and everyone in the reception area ran up to them. Mario was about to have his own heart attack and his cocaine high had completely faded and he had just bitched out on his boy upstairs. Self-loathing can't get any worse ... until it does. When it does, an old Saudi man latches on to you so you can make full-on eye contact with him as he dies from a vehement heart attack.

And that was how I found out I couldn't go anywhere without running into someone Potter hadn't fucked.

The most expensive date ever

One of the times Tinder came through ended up the most expensive weekend I had in the Middle East. I had matched with an older Filipino lady. We chatted for days and got along well. I told her I wanted to cook her dinner. She worked as a waitress in Bahrain so I thought cooking for her would be a nice change.

I rented a two-bedroom in Bahrain because it had an oven and a stove. I had to go over Thursday because that was the only day the booze shops were open and she said she liked to drink rum. Our date was Friday. Thursday, Waseem picked me up. Private taxi to Bahrain one-way, 300 riyal. Booze shop – wine, beers and a bottle of rum – 600 riyal. Grocery store – steak, bacon, salad, veggies, roses, various cooking supplies – 700 riyal. Two nights in a suite with a kitchen, 1,800 riyal.

Thursday night some friends came over and we drank and partied which was good use of the room. The next day I was prepping the meal all afternoon. She came over around seven and I greeted her with roses. She said she had never been given flowers before. Guys, give girls flowers. We went upstairs to my room, the table was already set, candles, music. Mind you I hadn't had a real date in over a year so I wanted to go all out. I made bacon sushi. You crisscross bacon and bake it in the oven, dice cherry tomatoes and lettuce and a dash of mayo, sprinkle with serrated cheddar and roll, slice and wah-lah bacon sushi.

The dinner spread was stellar. After dinner, we listened to YouTube and went back and forth with our music tastes. I played a lot of Lovage that night. Shout out to Dan the Automater! We talked about our various countries' holidays. It was nice. Was the first date I had been on in years, since I lived in Bangkok.

Things went great; we migrated to the bedroom, kissed each other goodbye the next morning. The room, the booze, the food and the taxis totalled over $1300. Dating hurts in the Middle East. Fuck does it hurt. The alternatives were masturbation or Chinese hookers, if that's your thang. Chinese hookers were not my thing so masturbation it was.

Jersey tries to come back

Everything you do in KSA is linked to your visa. If you have a real deal iqama visa EVERYTHING IS LINKED to it. Your phone, your internet, your driver's license, your job, anything.

Jersey had about a year off work post gold trip. He travelled around the world visiting friends and looking at ugly broncos to buy and refurbish. I was able to get him hired on at my current company. It was a dice roll as he had left the country in kind of a grey legal fog, so to speak. His credit cards were maxed out and unpaid. His Saudi rental car had been left at the Bahrain airport and his final month's rent at the trailer park was unpaid.

Jersey tried to contact the bank prior to coming back to set up some payment plan (that he would purposely fail at) but it was impossible. He called them, he emailed them. The Saudis were so fucked about doing any semblance of work that no one could be bothered. When Jersey finally got through to someone on the phone the guy didn't even know what to tell him.

Jersey: "I'm trying to pay my credit card bill but I'm no longer in KSA."

Saudi: "Hmmmmmmm."

That's as far as it got, a hmmmmmm. LOL, oh silly Saudis. To this day he still gets Happy (insert Muslim holiday) emails from that bank. Yes.

We had deduced that if there was anything on him regarding a file or inclusion on an 86'd list that it would have been linked to his old iqama and passport. So he got a new passport, which changed his passport number. We were fairly confident he could come back in. If they tried to call him out on his credit card he had an email trail of attempts at trying to fix it. He could also say he was coming back to pay it. It was highly unlikely though that they would be angry about credit card debt. A co-worker of Jersey's had over $200k in credit card debt that he dipped on, returned a year later and did the same thing. Paid for two of his kids to go through private school in Japan. As far as the Saudis were concerned, credit card debt was a made-up western concept like women's rights or freedom of speech.

Jersey arrived at Dammam airport and wasn't allowed in by immigration. They had introduced biometric scanners to which any entry or exit was now linked. His previous company had blocked his return. Had they blocked it because he had $60,000+ in credit card debt linked to their company? No. Had they blocked him because police came to their office about a bill that was due for his previous residence? No. Had they blocked him because the police came to their office a second time regarding a missing rental car? No.

He was blocked for two years because he didn't do his final exit properly. To do your final exit, your company had to go through all your paperwork. They gave you your final paycheck / bonus. Checked your Ps and Qs like outstanding credit card debt, due rent, utilities, etc. He had managed to get his final bonus without doing his final exit visa correctly though.

So, Jersey - 1, KSA - 1, but now he was stuck at the airport. They put him in a room and said he wasn't allowed to enter the country because of his last exit. A company can throw up a "complaint" against you if you leave your contract early or if you dip on them early, regardless if you do your final exit or not, if you leave on bad terms they can fuck you for working in KSA for life. So immigration told him sorry, but you can't come back in for at least two more years. He could leave KSA, it just had to be through that airport. There weren't any ticket booking desks, even outside the terminals. He sat in this room trying to figure out how to book a ticket. There was no Wi-Fi then in Saudi airports. No restaurants he could go to. There was a young Egyptian giving him the fuck-me eyes and Jersey put on his best samesies performance, got the guy's phone, booked a ticket out and then gave him Potter's number in place of his own.

Hospitals in KSA

Hospitals were the one place you could go and talk to women in KSA. They were filled with Filipino nurses. I had only been to a hospital in KSA once before, when my back was injured. No fun story there, woke up and couldn't move my neck. Was in horrible pain. Went to a hospital where they gave me some nice drugs and muscle relaxers.

This time I was going to get a hordeolum removed from my eye. I had been in Japan when the Tohoku earthquake hit. It was an awful experience. The world basically ended for three days. An earthquake of 9.1, a tsunami and a radioactive meltdown. I ended up going to Fukushima several times after the disaster to do relief work. Not too long after that I started to get terrible styes on my eyes. My lipids were no longer creating tears properly that would clean my eyes out and get rid of dirt. My lipids (small holes on the end of your eyelid) would clog and then inside my lids, horedeaulums would form. They were so bad I had to get them surgically removed. I've had this surgery in Japan, Thailand, and now KSA. KSA was the worst.

I went in to see the eye specialist. He was an Egyptian man. Great English. He looked at it and says ok tomorrow morning we cut. The next day I rolled back in and was ready. The worst thing about eye surgery is you have to watch it the entire time. You watch the needle come at you and into your eyelid for the

Novocain. You watch the scalpel. If you move your eye at all in the wrong direction you're blind. It's a very unnerving process. I don't recommend it. Every country has its own style when lancing a hordeolum. Saudi was the worst. The Egyptian did a fine job but after he was done he bandaged up my eye, then put his elbow billowing down on it for four minutes. No idea why he was doing this. "The pressure is good for the eye, my dear," he said.

Not so sure about that, doc. Blood started running down out of my eye onto my cheek. It was finally over and I was sitting in a chair with my eye all bandaged up, listening to the following days' procedures for medicine, rest, etc. My eye started to swell and throb with pain. The left side of my body was now in what I can only describe as shock. I told him there was severe pain going on. He said oh yeah the Novocain is probably wearing off. I could now feel every slice he made inside my eyelid and it fucking sucked. It was such a precise, concentrated pain I hope you never experience it, reader.

"Doc, you gunna do anything about this pain?" I asked.

"Oh you want pain medication? Does it hurt?" he asked.

YES IT FUCKING HURTS, generally when you cut open the inside of people's eyelids it fucking hurts. Finally he sent me to the anaesthetist where I was given me a shot in the ass and some shitty Arab pain pills. Four days of bed rest was nice, especially with two of those in Bahrain.

Don't ever give the finger to a Saudi (in KSA)

A friend of Jersey's had been working at the Navy for a company for a while. He worked with Jersey up in Rasta Nora, then when that company had a reduction in force he came down to Al Khobar. This man, we'll call him Oklahoma, was famous in our province. So famous that defence contractors all over the country had to rewrite their Saudi culture human resource guides to discuss road rage and hand gestures.

Oklahoma was driving with a friend down a pretty popular street in Dammam. A Saudi cut him off. Now, you will never ever imagine how bad these drivers are unless you go there. I am writing this book from a war zone elsewhere in the Middle East, where I've been bombed with motors and suicide bombers several times. KSA is 1,000 times scarier than here. Why? Because of the drivers and driving. There's a highway in KSA called Death Highway because your chances of dying on it are about 1 in 5. These fuckin clowns were literally the worst at everything in life.

So this Saudi driver cut Oklahoma off, causing him to rear off into the side bank, but still maintain his car and course. Once back on the road Oklahoma gave him the finger nice and loud out his car window. The Saudi then motioned for him to pull over. Oklahoma is about six foot and 325 pounds. This Saudi wasn't about to do dick to him. They pulled over and immediately started swinging at each other. They both got hits in, then it was over. The Saudi's friend called the police. The police came and arrested Oklahoma. As he was getting arrested the Saudi leans over to him and said, "I am going to end you over here, you will never go home."

Oklahoma was taken to jail and spent two nights there before he was bailed out by his company. His passport was taken. He wasn't allowed to leave the country until his trial. This shit took forever. It was delayed and delayed and delayed. Months into Oklahoma waiting, he kept good spirits but was very shaken. He had heard he would be getting a little jail time and lashes. Ninety lashes is what the judge told him. In addition to about a $25,000 fine. The Saudi claimed that Oklahoma tried to run him over, attempted vehicular homicide. One day at work I heard yelling down the hall. Our programme manager kicked Oklahoma off the base and sent him home to our compound. Once home, the programme manager sent over his H.R. bitch to tell Oklahoma he had been fired and had to leave the compound. Oklahoma now had no job, nowhere to live, no health insurance and he couldn't leave the country.

Luckily the manager of our compound had sympathy and a soul, unlike our programme manager, and hooked Oklahoma up with a small unit in a compound nearby. For the next year Oklahoma lived in this little closet. He would regularly go to the American consulate to attempt to get help to expedite his case. They did fuck all to help him. FUCK. ALL.

On and on this went. We contacted state representatives for him. I told him to write to Oprah. He was just so fucked. No job, couldn't legally work, no passport. Just stuck overseas waiting for lashes that kept getting delayed and delayed. We told him to call the consulate and threaten suicide. We all were extremely worried about him because he wore the depression thick. It was a really dark time for him and it was about to get darker. He had no end sight of leaving, his mom was in the hospital, he had been fired, he had no job, no insurance ... an awful scenario I wouldn't ever wish on any person.

There are several things that are absolute no-nos in every country you visit. KSA has lots. Sharia law is law and always will be in KSA. In most Muslim countries tattoos are taboo, if not illegal altogether. Oklahoma had a tattoo on the lower part of his leg. This was a problem not because of him having a tattoo. Plenty of foreign workers had tattoos over there and it was not a problem. This was a problem because of what Oklahoma's tattoo said. There are daily Arabic phrases everyone uses in KSA as well as elsewhere in the Middle East. The absolute most common one heard and said is "Inshallah". This translates to "God-willing" or "If God wills it". You will hear this everyday guaranteed.

Oklahoma had this phrase tattooed on the bottom part of his leg in Arabic. When you live abroad you are exposed to a variety of expats, as you've now read, and often the expats will really do some shit that makes your head literally shake and you say to yourself, "what ... the ... fuck".

This was insanely idiotic to do and I still close my eyes and shake my head at it. The problem here is that he now had the word GOD in Arabic tattooed on his person, right by his foot. The feet are considered the lowest part of the body when it comes to Asian culture and their association with religion and spiritualism. This is true from Buddhism to Islam. Islamic law in KSA was so strict when it came to anything to do with God that reproduced images of any person were considered haram because they could be associated with idolatry. Needless to say, getting anything with the word Allah in it tattooed on your person is a horrible idea if you are living in a Muslim country, especially if it is located near your foot. Oklahoma had been kicked out of several restaurants after the locals saw this tattoo. The police even came to a restaurant once and forced him to leave because of it, but only after scolding him repeatedly.

Now he was faced with lashing and jail time. Both punishments would require him to be naked in front of the authorities. He also would be dealing with cellmates most of whom would be Muslims. He had no idea what reactions he would get from this but he knew they would not be good. He had to get the tattoo removed by any means possible before serving his sentence. He had spent several years in the Philippines and could speak a variety of Filipino dialects. There's a large community of Filipino workers in KSA and he went to them for help. He eventually made his way to an underground Filipino tattoo parlour in our province, in the city of Al Khobar. Tattoo parlours were illegal and haram in KSA. Well, Oklahoma found a good one and they changed the Arabic writing to a chain of camels all linked together.

That solved one problem. He was still faced with ninety lashes and no date in sight of when he would be able to leave. When I left KSA he was still there waiting his fate …

Over a year after his arrest I got a message from Jersey saying Oklahoma got out. "How the fuck did he get out!!!!!" I asked. "He went to see the prince!" says Jersey.

The Prince and the house plant

Oklahoma had been in Saudi purgatory for over a year. He finally had enough of dealing with dead answers and empty promises from the consulate and the police. He went to a hardware store and bought a house plant. He then took a taxi with the house plant to a royal building where he heard the province's prince worked out of.

He walked up to the receptionist and said he needed to talk to the prince. The receptionist laughed at him so Oklahoma said he would wait. After thirty minutes the receptionist told him he would not get to see the prince. Oklahoma started explaining to the receptionist why it was so important for him to meet the prince and said he would not leave until he did. A man walked out of the back room and asked what was going on. Oklahoma explained he was stuck in the country and nobody was doing anything about it and he had to see the prince. The man then said, "Ok, my dear, come with me." He escorted Oklahoma to a back room where he sat for about an hour. Another man, the prince's secretary, then came out and asked him what he needed to see the prince for and why he was carrying a house plant. Oklahoma explained his situation and told him the plant was a gift for the prince. The secretary said wait one minute. Finally another man came out and said, "Sir, please follow me." They went through several doors and into a room where the prince was sitting, waiting for him.

"How can I help you? " asked the prince.

Oklahoma explained his predicament and that he was stuck in KSA with no help from anyone. All the while his mother was in the hospital in the States with no one to care for her.

The prince nodded for a minute then asked what tribe the man from the altercation was from. Oklahoma told him and the prince laughed. "Habibi, that tribe is no nonsense, that's the worst tribe to get into a road rage incident with. You are forgiven, my son. You will not go to jail and you will not owe anyone anything anymore. But, as for your visa, I do not have power over your overstay, you must pay immigration whatever you owe them then you are free to go, my child."

Oklahoma was in tears at this point. He thanked the prince, gave him the house plant, and went straight to immigration. Oklahoma was home within a week. He also held no ill feelings towards the Saudis after this, he was more disappointed with how the Americans at his company and at the consulate had dealt with the situation.

Mario and the police

Mario and I went over to Bahrain for a day of drinking. We weren't going to spend the night because we wanted to save money. I called up one of my friends in Bahrain and asked if she could get us beers. It was a Friday and the beer store was closed so we were at her mercy. She said should could find us beer and we could drink at her place. We hopped in a cab and rolled over. I still can't remember what kind of beer she got us but it was mad strong and had a very high alcohol content. We crushed a case and were blind drunk. Mario passed out on the couch. We woke up around 5 pm and left to go get food as we were still far too drunk to be in a taxi and go across the causeway. We made it to Bennigan's but I was just too fucked up to be there so I told Mario I was getting a room at Al Jabriya and I passed out there. Mario had caught his second wind and continued drinking at Bennigan's, saying he would meet me later.

Next morning I woke up and Mario hadn't come to the room. I messaged him several times and called his phone but no dice. I went back to sleep. I woke up and it was now almost noon and Mario was still nowhere to be found. I messaged Jesse and told him what was going on, asked if he'd heard from Mario. He hadn't. More scrambling, messaging mutual friends that he might have bumped into the previous night. Nothing. It was now nearly 2 o'clock and I had to check out. At 1:55 Mario came busting in the room. "Dude, I literally almost got arrested this morning, the fucking police woke me up." Mario had a huge open cut on his forehead.

So what had happened to Mario? He'd stayed drinking at Bennigan's and continued to increase his levels of inebriation. He ended up passing out at the bar and cracking his head on the bar floor rail. He was then kicked out of Bennigan's for being too drunk. He tried to find Al Jabriya but couldn't. Al Jabriya hotel was literally next door to Bennigan's. You walked out, turned right and walked 200 feet and that's it. We'd done this millions of times before but that night he was just too fucked.

Mario started going into random condo buildings behind Bennigan's. He then fell asleep on a couch in one of them in their reception area. The receptionist apparently tried to wake him several times and he wasn't havin it. The receptionist called the police. The police came and tried to wake him. No luck. They then slapped him in the face to wake him, at which point he woke for a split second and said, "Fuck off already." That was enough. The police grabbed him up and put cuffs on him and threw him in the back of their car. He had no idea what was going on.

After driving about two blocks he snapped back to reality. The police were telling him "You are going to jail". Mario pleaded with them that it was all a misunderstanding and that he was just trying to find his hotel. He begged them to stop at a hotel so he could get a room to sleep in. Surprisingly they let him try but told him he only had one chance. He went into Al Mansour Hotel and the police followed him. He asked for a room and got one. Apologized to the police and slept. This must have been around 5-6 am ish. Mario – 1, Police – 0.

Wearing a gay man's pants

Jesse and I headed over in his whip to Bahrain for drinking one weekend. I had matched with a super-hot girl on Tinder and planned on meeting her later that evening. Jesse would no doubt strike empty on Grindr and sit in his hotel bedroom alone. Bless his heart.

The girl was from Lebanon and was super fucking hot. We met for dinner and hit it off. She wanted to go out and party. Now, I do not have any fashion sense whatsoever. I tend to wear crocs and dress in slightly above-pyjama standards. This date wasn't any acceptation. However, once we decided we'd go clubbing afterwards, this presented a problem.

We got to the club. It was a place I'd never been before. The bouncers took one look at me, shook their heads and said "no way". Closed toe shoes and dress pants. I was in Thai fisherman cloth shorts and crocs and a white tee. I looked at my date and shrugged my shoulders. She said she wanted to dance and told me she would hit me up after the club. As I walked away I called up Jesse. "Jesse, dude, emergency, the super-hot Lebanese girl I'm out with, she wants me to go to a club with her, but I don't have the clothes, can I borrow some?" Jesse laughed and asked me if I've seen his clothes before. "Yes, Jesse, I have but I really want to fuck this girl. Can I come check out what you got?"

I arrived at his hotel and looked through his clothes. He had one pair of skinny jeans and some ugly pointy dress shoes. I hugged him and ran back to the club. Homegirl was so happy to see me she ran up, jumped on me and kissed me. We danced all night and had breakfast the next morning.

Rakim

Al Jabriya had a sister hotel directly next to it called the Al Commodore. The Al Commodore was the exact same layout as Al Jabriya, just 30% smaller. It was also 30% cheaper. Mario and

I started using it as our crash pad when partying in Bahrain. At about 10 pm, if we were able, we would part ways and go hunt ass. He being a samesie and me looking for opposites, we didn't hunt together but after getting our booty we would then regroup back at the hotel. Other times we would just get wasted at the Al Commodore and blast early 90s rap.

One particular night I got very excited and decided to throw furniture. An ironing board may or may not have been thrown down a hallway. The hotel had an ironing board set up in the small hallway of the room. I kept walking into it or rather it kept bumping me every time I walked through the hallway and I guess I had had enough after about the seventeenth time I bumped into it. This stupid ironing board broke a massive glass table top. I awoke the next morning to find a huge cracked piece of glass on the floor. Like five foot by six foot. I asked Mario what happened, he laughed and told me about my ironing board Olympics. What are we gonna do with this glass? I looked in one of the bedrooms and say it'll fit under the bed's mattress.

We lift up the mattress and take both broken pieces and put them under the mattress. Made up the bed and swept up the remaining pieces of glass. Problem solved. Months later we were back in the same room. We checked under the mattress and the glass was still there! It lasted there for over seven months. Oh, Al Commodore, you keep it classy.

Last Qatar flight outta KSA

Ramadan was upon us. Jersey and I were going to hit the Philippines. Having not been allowed back into KSA, Jersey pissed around Bangkok for a couple of months and waited for me to arrive. I had booked a month-long trip in Cebu, Philippines, to study Kali / Escrima. Escrima is a Filipino martial art that consists of close-quarter knife and stick fighting. I grew up studying it with my brother and father and was super excited to study more in its birthplace.

My buddy Fox and I are in the airport in Dammam both flying out for Ramadan. We are on the same flight, 11 pm DMM to Doha, Qatar. It was delayed by about two hours. We finally boarded the flight, it was now 1 am. We sat on the plane at the gate for another two hours after boarding. Mechanical issues. We finally taxied out then the engines stopped, another two hours we finally got off the runway and back towards the gate and they told us to disembark.

Now this presented a problem. KSA had no system in place for this. There were no Qatar crew members to accompany people off the plane or any airport staff to guide anyone. We got off near-ish the gate and walked back to the airport to the only entrance that there seemed to be. It took us upstairs to the other side of security. All three hundred of us were standing around wondering what the fuck to do. After about thirty minutes, we started to cattle ourselves through immigration again.

We are all standing around waiting and there was no one telling us anything. People were on their phones calling Qatar airlines, some were leaving to try and catch other flights in Bahrain. It was a complete mess.

Finally, around 6 am, a Qatar airways guy came over and made an announcement. He could have never been less prepared for the outrage he received. Since there were hundreds of us we could barely hear him. We finally got him to stand on a chair to address us. He said the flight has been cancelled and he had no further information.

I've never seen three hundred pissed-off people before. It's not a great sight. This poor guy ... But fuck Qatar for dropping the ball this hard. Everyone was yelling at him and it was basically thirty minutes of bitching at one guy who didn't cause the problem and had no way to give us updates. He asked us to be patient and left. He came back hours later and said that there would be another flight at 11 am and we would probably be on that one. He would come back with tickets later in the morning.

Here's why this was so fucked. 30% of the people on this flight were on their exit visa. They couldn't leave the airport and really shouldn't have been allowed back in. If you wanted to, you could have left and gone home to sleep but not if your visa was on final exit. So there were about two hundred and fifty of us sleeping in Dammam's ghetto-ass gate entrance hallway restaurant area.

By restaurant area I mean a Popeye's and a coffee shop. Both of which were closed. I tried to get some sleep but it wasn't really happening.

At around 9:30 am the guy came back with all the tickets in his hand. There were, like I said, over two hundred and fifty people. This fool, bless his little heart, tried to stand in the middle of us all and call out people's names. His voice carried about four foot at best. I walked through the crowd and grabbed the tickets, thanked him for his time and started calling out names. Strangely enough I got a round of applause. I was murdering half these names as there was a mix of foreign nationals from all over the world. I was reading speedily and it was going quick. I finally got to my name, which was like one of the last fifty. I said I'm done and handed the rest of the tickets to someone else and headed to my gate to try and catch what little sleep I was able to.

The Middle East cock blocks Qatar

Within a day of arriving in Bangkok I got an email from Qatar saying all flights into KSA for the future were to be cancelled until further notice. Several countries in the Middle East did a full-on blockade on Qatar. They said it was because Qatar was funnelling money to the Taliban and other terrorist organizations. Really, guys? Would have been more believable had you said you were blockading them because their football team had better goalies.

Took me forever with Qatar but I eventually got them to refund my ticket back to KSA. Wouldn't have been so hard pressed up, but after the debacle I went through trying to get out, and how poorly they handled our cancelled flight in Dammam, I was determined to get every single dinar I could squeeze out of them, deservingly so.

Malina to Palawan

Jersey and I were on an overnight ferry from Manila to Palawan. From Palawan we would take a bus then another ferry to Coron for diving. The ferry was massive. There were two levels with about four hundred sleeper bunks on each level. There was also a small back room with nicer VIP bunks. I opted for the VIP bunk, which was $4 more. Jersey is pretty tight with his monies so he was happy to slum it in the general bedding area.

Their guitar skills and singing skills may be some of the best in the world but the food in the Philippines is awful. They eat half-developed bird foetuses in their eggs. Their culinary senses are fucked. Have you ever heard of Jollibee? It's a Filipino fast-food chain. They have them in the Philippines and in KSA. The only reason they are in KSA is because of the huge amount of Filipino expats working in the kingdom. Here's a Jollibee meal. Chopped up hotdog pieces in mayonnaise and hot sauce. Fucking vomit.

The food on the ferry was no different. We went to the restaurant and looked at the menu and said no thanks.

On the top deck you could look out over the South China Sea, which like most large bodies of water was openly definitive and immensely calming. Long open distances with the rhythmic blue motions of the water are always a sort of nature's benzo for me. Gazing out to endless oceans and seas is a very ego dissolving experience.

I heard some ruckus from around a hallway deck and walked over. There hunched down were about five older Filipino gentleman gambling on two fighting cocks. Wow. Cock fighting on a ferry. I went and got Jersey and told him to look around the corner. Laughs for days.

Coron, once there, was absolutely beautiful. We went diving and beaching. Caught some bad sunburn and were both bedridden for days. We finally made our way to Cebu.

Cebu bounce

We stayed at an apartment in Cebu city. Cebu is pretty gritty and grimy. The island itself has some world famous waterfalls and a large population of whale sharks to the south. I was there to study Eskrima at Doce Pares. This island is the birthplace of Escrima and famous in the martial arts world.

After two weeks of being on Cebu, Tinder was at an all-time high. I met a girl for a movie and dinner. We hit if off and ended up back at my place. The next morning I got a call from Jersey.

"Get that girl the fuck outta your room and let's get to the beach, pronto."

Laughing I said ok and to gimmie ten. I showered, told homegirl I gotta bounce and we could link up later. My phone rang again, "What's up, Jersey?"

"BAE just called me. I'm going Iraq. Come down and get your money, I'm out," said Jersey.

BAE is the mother of all contractors. We had both been trying to get on with their contract in Iraq as specialists. All we knew was that the Iraq contract wasn't KSA and it paid over $9k a month. I literally almost dropped my phone. I ran down stairs and met Jersey. "DUDE! You got it!!!! How, when, etc?" The fellas that interviewed me for this job interviewed him that morning. They told him to pack a bag and get moving. I was still waiting on an offer of employment. I bade Jersey farewell and went back to my phone and emailed the recruiter I had been dealing with.

> Dear Mr —
> Please allow me to clarify that I am immediately ready to start at your convenience. Please let me know if there is anything I can do to expedite this process.

Within six hours I received a reply.

Dear Mr —
If you can be in USA by this Friday you have a job.

Looked at homegirl and told her I was leaving that night.
We will have to continue this affair another time, darling.

Kayak, I love you

I got on my phone and started booking ticket after ticket. Here was my flight plan: Cebu to Manila, ticket 1. Manila to Bangkok, ticket 2. Bangkok to Bahrain, ticket 3. Taxi to KSA to get my shit then taxi back to Bahrain. Bahrain to Paris, ticket 4. Paris to Pittsburgh, ticket 5. I left that same night and had very short layovers in between each flight. I had hit up a hospital in Cebu and had got some Xanax and a script. I had to take about seven flights in twenty-four hours. Was gonna need some Xannies for these flights. Did a test for TB, which they quarantine me for. Fuckin hell, hospitals abroad are shady like timeshares.

I landed in Bahrain. Waseem picked me up. "Waseem!!! I'm leaving Saudi!" I happily explained. I had my entire studio at this time in my second bedroom. I packed a bag of clothes and my

DJ-mixer. Everything else I packed up and put in Jesse's room. If I didn't pass the medical or didn't get the job in Iraq then I'd be coming back. There was a massive long hiring process that required a lengthy background check and extreme medical check. If I did pass everything, I'd figure out what the fuck to do with all this shit once in Iraq. By then I'd have the cash to fly over and pick it up or have it mailed or thrown out. Whichever was easiest. I packed it all up and put it in Jesse's room. Jesse was going to try and stay in KSA over Ramadan, which he ended up not doing, very good idea. I got in his room and he had left in such a hurry there was a hair clipper laying on the floor, still on, buzzing away. Three hours, twelve boxes, four turntables, three hundred records later, I was done moving.

I had two big jugs of wine cooking I had to dump in one of the showers. That was sad 'cos they smelled like they were gunna be some nice tasty batches. I called Waseem and headed across the causeway for quite possibly the last time ever.

Once back in the States, I did the crazy physical and awaited the contract to be awarded. Two months of eating peperoni pizza and drinking beer was great. Gained about twenty pounds. Got to see my family and friends, got to see The Avalanches and Aesop Rock and Phish. Come August I finally got the call. Mr — please be ready for contractor training at Ft. bliss in El Paso Thursday. FUCK YES.

Juarez

During military training in El Paso, Texas, I tried to find someone to cross the border into Juarez with me but nobody would. I was so close to the border I wasn't going to miss the chance. Found a taxi on base and took it to the border crossing and walked into Mexico. After all the hype I didn't find it that dangerous although this was in the middle of the day. Manila is far sketchier in the daytime than Juarez. Popped into a pharmacy and checked out the locale Xanax prices for my global-pharmaceutical-economic-price-listings-index (prices were ok). Walked around town and went into some guitar shops trying to source some vinyl but no luck. Walked around a cathedral and watched some street ceremonies. Time for drinks. Found a bar. Sucked down three beers and ordered a set of tacos. Soaking up the atmosphere in Juarez by myself was the perfect ending to my time in Saudi Arabia and a marker to start what would be my time in Iraq. As I ordered another beer I thought to myself of Hunter S. Thompson's "place of definitions". Crossing borders, travelling in dangerous places, getting visas for countries that most can't, going to places where people say not to go, befriending people Fox news would have you believe wanted to kill you ... all these things made my blood feel alive, like it was circulating in the place of definitions. The cook came out and he was wearing your usual wife-beater shirt and dirty apron. I looked up and he had an eyepatch on.

Fuck, yes. My first time in Mexico and I was in Juarez (homicide capital of Mexico, "Sicario", etc.) and my cook who brought me my tacos had an eyepatch. It couldn't get more real than this. On to the next.

MUAMMAR EMKA

JAKARTA UNDER COVER

Indonesia's Bestselling Nonfiction Series

MUAMMAR EMKA

JAKARTA UNDER COVER II

Indonesia's Bestselling Nonfiction Series

EWE PAIK LEONG

KUALA LUMPUR UNDER COVER

EWE PAIK LEONG

KUALA LUMPUR UNDER COVER II

Includes Bangkok, Batam and Karimun Island

MALCOLM SCOTT

BALI UNDER COVER

Sequel to the international bestseller Bali Raw

EWE PAIK LEONG

PENANG UNDER COVER

Includes Batam, Bangkok and Kuala Lumpur

EWE PAIK LEONG

PATTAYA UNDER COVER

Includes Bangkok, Saigon and KL

HARPER WALSH

SAUDI ARABIA UNDER COVER

Includes Bahrain, Bangkok and Cairo